ONE DECISION AWAY

ONE DECISION AWAY

KEY PRINCIPLES
TO CREATE WHAT YOU WANT
IN LIFE AND WORK

PAULA MELO DOROFF

NEW DEGREE PRESS

COPYRIGHT © 2022 PAULA MELO DOROFF

ONE DECISION AWAY

Key Principles to Create What You Want in Life and Work

ISBN   979-8-88504-286-4   *Hardcover*

I DEDICATE THIS BOOK TO:

*My grandmother, Maria, who taught me how
to be tough and have faith in God.*

*My aunt, Grace, who taught me about
generosity and love of great food.*

*My uncle, Anthony, who taught me about the power
of giving someone your undivided attention.*

Paul and Esther for their love and support.

Mara and Carmem for their commitment toward my family and me.

*Every single employer who gave me an opportunity and
saw qualities in me that I did not even see in myself.*

My mentors, coaches, and teachers—you know who you are.

My dear friends who make me feel so loved, you are like family to me.

*My husband, Randy, who is an example of
living a life of integrity and consistency.*

*My sons, Carlo and Enzo, who allow me to love them
the way I always wanted to be loved every day.*

The Doroff Family who wholeheartedly welcomed me into their lives.

The United States of America, the country of my dreams.

All who have served this great country in any capacity.

*My birth mother, Helena, who birthed me and taught me
that being alive was a gift worth having after all.*

*Above all, I dedicate this book to God. He who never abandoned
me and always guided and protected me through it all.*

CONTENTS

———

FOREWORD

———

"One Decision Away" is about determination, not determinism. Determinism suggests that the individual we are was "caused" by our ancestors, our grandparents, our parents, our environment. Your author disagrees with that. She acknowledges all of those factors "influence" who we are, but they do not "cause" who we are.

"One Decision Away" is about one's freedom to choose. If my grandparents and parents were child abusers (which they weren't by the way), that does not mean I must be a child abuser also. I can make a different choice. Being angry with my child doesn't "cause" me to strike her. Between my anger and my response, I have time to think and to "choose" not to strike. I am just one decision away from not being abusive. I can choose to e-think-motion (a term I made up).

Paula's own story and the stories of the people you will meet in this book offer proof that every decision matters; that regardless of our past and our current circumstance we can make a decision to change our today and to create our tomorrow.

This book is inspiring, and by that I mean it is in-spirit-a-tional. The principles Paula shares are principles of our spirit. They aren't found outside of ourselves. They are found inside of ourselves. "One Decision Away" will inspire its readers to be proactive; Stephen R Covey's first habit of highly effective people, versus reactive.

Paula's words inspired me to decide what to think about and to think about my thoughts and actions. I have the freedom to choose my thoughts and actions. I have the freedom to choose personal growth, to choose to value people (including myself), to choose to be kind, to choose to be forgiving of others and myself, to choose to be grateful, to choose to heal.

Writing this book took an act of courage on Paula's part. The decisions Paula made to change her life, and the decisions made by the people whose stories you will read in the following pages, required courage. Courage is what is needed to effectively face fear. Most of us admire courageous people, and we even desire to be courageous ourselves. Unfortunately, absent fear there is no courage. Fearless people are not courageous. They are fearless. Paula Doroff is not fearless. She is courageous.

Readers, it's our turn to be courageous. After all, we're just "One Decision Away."

DOUG LENNICK,
CEO AND CO-FOUNDER OF THINK2PERFORM
AND AUTHOR OF *MORAL INTELLIGENCE*
AND *FINANCIAL INTELLIGENCE*

INTRODUCTION

"Go with God," she said ten years earlier. On that day, I packed my bags and ran away forever.

Was God still with me now? I wondered while I was in the arrival's bathroom of Logan International Airport.

I was twenty-five years old and utterly overwhelmed; the very instant the plane had landed in America, I started to cry uncontrollably. But now that we had left the plane, I was alone, tears drying, unable to tell if it was relief or sheer exhaustion I was feeling. I stared blankly at my face in the mirror, and it dawned on me just how big a step I had taken.

I had done it.

Yes, just outside the bathroom doors lay one of the scariest frontiers I would ever contend with: immigration. Stern officials would be waiting in booths to look me over, inspect my papers, and ultimately decide whether I was good enough to be let in. They could take one look at me and see how unworthy I was to pass through the gates, on the other side of which lay all my dreams.

"Paula, you can do this. Just smile. Take deep breaths…"

Although I felt very much alone in that moment, the truth was I wasn't. I *had* gone with God, just like my grandmother had told me to years ago. God was there with me that day, walking me through to the other side of that line, holding my hand with every step I took.

I walked toward immigration, taking yet another terrifying jump from the known into the unknown. I knew then, and know even more deeply now, that when you chase your dreams, every step you take is a giant leap.

Crossing thresholds is something I've been doing my whole life. Between running away from my small hometown in Brazil at fifteen and arriving in the United States at twenty-five, I had already lived in three countries and married three times. I grew up in poverty, my birth parents were never part of my life, and I was raised by an illiterate grandmother who never once showed me an ounce of affection.

I had nothing more than a middle school education, and I know firsthand what it means to never feel good enough, smart enough, or talented enough. I have battled depression and anxiety that strangled my soul like a cancer. I hid my past like a shameful secret, convinced I'd never be seen as good enough if people knew my real story.

Most people believe that where you start out in your journey determines your final destination. They think your success comes down to your family, your lucky breaks, or your wealth, but that's not always true. I am proof of that.

Growing up, I had nothing except a dream. Nobody would have predicted that someone like me would live the life I've lived. But I had seen a handful of hardworking Brazilians escape, and I wanted the same for myself. I broke free from my painful childhood beginnings and found my way to America, the country I had grown up dreaming about.

Over the past few decades, I carved out my own unlikely path to success on Wall Street, in arguably one of the most male-dominated industries of all: financial services. I overcame a very difficult past, found my voice, and breathed life into a future that nobody expected of me.

Let me ask, where are *you* right now?

If you're anything like the average American, research is now showing you're probably experiencing depression, anxiety, or an overall feeling of being "stuck."

A 2021 study in *The Lancet* found that global rates of depression are now at an all-time high, with increasing post-COVID-19 anxiety levels impacting millions of people's lives (Santomauro et. al., 2021). The National Alliance on Mental Illness (NAMI) claims that one in five American adults experienced mental illness in 2020, which is almost 53 million people.

Similarly, the National Center for Health Statistics (NCHS) together with the Census Bureau found in 2020 that out of every one hundred US adults, thirty-four have experienced anxiety, depression, or both.

It's not just our personal lives that are suffering. A recent Gallup poll (Gallup, 2022) showed a measly 21 percent of people are engaged with and committed to their work. In 2021, *The Harvard Business Review* talked about the "Great Resignation" and cited a 20 percent increase in resignation rates from 2020 to 2021.

As a nation, we are burnt out at work and unhappy at home. Why?

I felt called to write this book because now, more than ever, people are stuck. They want to make changes because they know something is missing, and they want to find out what it is. Deep down, they know they don't want to "die with their music still in them," as Dr. Oliver Wendell Holmes once said (Brainyquote). So many people are living in pain, in their bodies, minds, and souls, and all they have is what I once had—a dream and the desire for more for themselves.

I know pessimism is fashionable these days, and everyone thinks that if you're dealt a bad hand, that's it for you. I want to assure you: I've walked those roads, and I've been down those paths. I want to share the maps I used to find my way out so that as many people as possible can achieve the same fulfillment and happiness that I now have.

I want to show you that you are just *one decision away* from completely altering the trajectory of your life. To make that step, I believe *courage* is the secret.

Courage is needed for you to take chances and leave your comfort zone. You need courage to drop your façade, release your shame, and speak your truth. You also need courage to face all those limiting stories you tell about who you are and what you're capable of, as well as the courage to rewrite those stories.

This book is for all those men and women who are ready and willing to take that leap and embrace change. Is that you?

No two lives are the same. But even if your story is nothing like mine, I believe that when it comes to major life transitions, people have far more in common than it seems. Whether you're in your twenties and just starting out or you're making big transitions after decades of life, there's something in this book for you.

Whoever you are, whether you're working in the corporate world or unemployed, currently living an abundant life, or just scraping by from paycheck to paycheck, the principles in this book can change the game for you. Whether you're feeling burnt out, uninspired, inauthentic, or just in limbo, I want to show you a new way forward—the same path I took on my long, long journey to get here.

I'm not the only one who has taken that journey. In the chapters that follow, I'll share the stories of seven incredible people who have overcome tremendous challenges of their own. Through personal one-on-one interviews, I was able to learn firsthand the strategies that worked for them. These very different people share something in common: They all stepped bravely into the unknown in their own unique ways.

You'll meet:

- A man who, against all odds, broke free from his troubled life on the streets of Los Angeles, managed to join the US Marines, graduated from an Ivy League school, and pieced together his dream career as a filmmaker and storyteller.
- A woman who grew up in Detroit in the sixties with drug dealers for parents and a teen pregnancy that threatened to derail her life. She is now a successful life coach inspiring and leading others.
- A brilliant and ultra-ambitious woman in her mid-thirties who battled obsessive-compulsive disorder (OCD), depression, and a broken engagement. She walked away from what she had always thought was her future. Today, she is the successful owner of several businesses, a social media star, and proud co-producer of her own TV show.
- A fifty-year-old who was abandoned by his mother on the streets of South Korea at just five years old. He lived in an orphanage until he was adopted by an American family, later becoming a US Marine and using those lessons of discipline to drive a successful corporate career.
- A woman in her thirties who grew up on food stamps with an abusive mother who brought a conveyor belt of equally abusive men into the home. Though plagued with health problems and post-traumatic stress disorder (PTSD), she eventually went on to work at Microsoft

and has transitioned to building her dream business as a life coach.

- A young man with an Iraqi-Jewish background who grew up with severe dyslexia but realized he would have to shake off the labels he'd been given and redefine himself. He would ultimately defy the odds and land a job in the world's most successful financial company.
- A brilliant forty-year-old entrepreneur and business coach who started life as a refugee during the Bosnian war. Today, she has built her life around her mission of sharing messages of peace, forgiveness, and the power of service to others.

I will be sharing the principles each of these inspiring individuals used to succeed, as well as the tools I learned from other incredible people who overcame their own adversity, including Nelson Mandela, Oprah Winfrey, and legendary hedge fund investor, Ray Dalio.

I believe that where you are in your life today is a very strong predictor of where you're heading, *unless you do something different*. This book will help you do just that. Together we'll explore:

- How to tap into your dreams and get clear on your goals
- How to create a realistic plan to achieve those goals
- What it really means to commit to a plan
- The single best investment you can make
- Why kindness *does* pay
- Why professional success without healing leads to unfulfillment
- How to identify self-sabotage (and how to change!)
- How to master the twin arts of gratitude and generosity

Real insight comes from lived experience. This book is not just about personal development or professional development, it is about both. Though inspirational, the principles we'll explore here are meant to be *applied,* step by step. It's only with inspired action that we shift from where we are to the possibilities of where we could be.

One decision could change the course of your entire life. If you have a dream, I want this book to give you courage. If you're at a crossroads, I want you to know that right now, you have the power to change everything. Achieving your dreams is within your grasp, and courageously crossing that threshold is only ever *one decision away.*

CHAPTER 1

GET CLEAR

"You want to die? Go ahead."

It was the voice of the person who ruled over my world, my grandmother, Maria. I stood there in the blazing Brazilian sun, just eight years old, as she gestured toward the busy road that spanned the front of our house.

I hated my life.

I hated myself.

I hated my birth mother for abandoning me when I was a baby and, even though I never met him, I hated my father for not coming to rescue me from it all.

One day, I'd been caught playing with a neighborhood child who my strict and uncompromising grandmother disapproved of. For daring to engage with someone of the wrong faith, my punishment was a fierce whipping in the front of our house. Face wet with tears, I glared at her and pronounced how utterly miserable I was and how all I wanted to do was die. That was when she said the words that still haunt me today. "You want to die? Go ahead."

I didn't die that day, but at that moment, something inside me did. I'll never know why I didn't have the courage to hurl myself in front of a truck back then, but the road became a symbol for me as a way out, a way to end my despair. Even though I didn't know it then, in a way, one day that road *would* save me.

My grandmother used to say I went to sleep with the chickens, which is an expression older people in Brazil still use to describe people who go to bed early. I went to bed early because bedtime was my refuge. Tucked away from the world under my blanket, I'd shut my eyes and vividly imagine the life of my dreams. I invented a life where I was surrounded by adults who loved me for who I was and friends who adored me, and I had a safe place I was proud to call home.

I would envision myself inside a plane, jetting far away to America. I wanted the life I'd seen in the old issues of glossy magazines the newsstand near me would throw away. I'd heard America was the place you made something of yourself, the place people like me could change their fate. I'd finally prove to my grandmother that I was *not* going to turn out like the young single mothers in our neighborhood—lost, hopeless, and relying on government help.

My grandmother had no belief in me, and it took me until adulthood to really understand why. Born into a family of thirteen in a rural farming community, she was never taught to read or write as she was never expected to do more than housework and child-rearing. In her twenties, an accident threw her husband off the back of a construction truck and onto the highway where he died instantly. She was young. She had two little kids, and she was eight months pregnant with her third child. A devout and hardworking woman, life conditioned her to be a woman of steel.

It's ironic how much I hated my grandmother in my childhood, and yet today, she is one of the people I love most. She taught me to be tough, and proving her wrong gave me a reason to fight. Her question that day was brutal, but it spurred me on: Did I really want to die? No, I wanted life more than anything! The life I fantasized about, alone in my bed at night—*that* was the life I wanted.

But the life I did have was empty.

In my life, there was no love, no hope, and no light. At just eight years old, my mission was crystal clear: I had to get out of there.

For years, I scrimped and saved and plotted my escape. I endured sexual abuse at the hands of a couple of people in my neighborhood, never-ending poverty, and my grandmother's utterly annihilating lack of love for me. Enough was enough. I had waited so long for my day of escape, and when it came at age fifteen, I didn't know what to do with myself.

After a restless night, I awoke to the heady smell of *café com leite,* the Brazilian coffee my grandmother would brew for us early each morning before school. The smell was the same as it ever was, but this morning, it was *me* who was different. Would I have the courage to follow through with my plan? What if my grandmother knew about my plot all along? What if she could sense my fear or read my secret thoughts about escaping?

I'd need to wind my way through the back streets and down to the bus stop I walked to every morning to catch the bus to work. Only this time, I had a different destination in mind. I'd take the bus to the *rodoviaria,* the only place you could get a bus out of state. I knew that for my life to change, I'd need to get on that bus and never look back. I'd been quietly gathering courage until the day I was brave enough to make the leap. Today was that day.

I can still remember the sickening fear I felt and the terror that my grand escape would just be a grand waste of time. I feared I'd be caught or I'd escape but fail out there anyway. What if I became homeless? What if I had to come back, tail between my legs, begging for shelter and food? Even worse, what if my grandmother was right and I was already on the path to failure she had so cruelly predicted for me?

Why would God help *me* succeed?

I can't tell you all the tiny steps that took me to that point and beyond it, but I do know that even if you have very little, you can work with it and create something valuable. Even small splinters of hope can save you.

DREAMS ARE NOT A LUXURY. THEY ARE A NECESSITY.
Before starting my own professional coaching business, I spent twenty-two years working with some of the largest financial companies in the world. I worked my way up

from an entry level position to vice president of investments. Clients would often tell me, "Dreams don't pay the bills." That might be what some people think, but my life is proof otherwise.

When I was ten years old, my grandmother taught me how to make rugs from leftover *retalhos,* or vibrantly colored fabric scraps. Using empty rice, bean, or sugar sacks, I'd make the rugs on the weekends. After school, I'd sell them door-to-door to the neighborhood moms for less than five dollars apiece. Like us, they were just trying to make ends meet, so I was lucky if I sold one rug per week.

One day, our neighbor's daughter, Patricia, came home after work and pulled me aside. "You know, I'll be having this baby soon. My boss asked me to find someone to cover for me during my maternity leave. I know you're making your rugs, but what if *you* cover for me?" I couldn't believe my ears. At the time, I was a thirteen-year-old girl who knew nothing about office work. Hell, I'd never even stepped inside an office, and she wanted me to do her job. My mind raced.

It was a receptionist job at a secondhand car dealership. Patricia said the work wouldn't be too hard. I just needed to sound mature and confident, and she'd train me to do things like answer the phone, handle messages, and write invoices. *Invoices?* I didn't even know what that meant. I was thrilled anyway. Was this how I would make my escape?

"My grandmother wouldn't let me. Never." It was like I spoke on autopilot. As quickly as it had come, my excitement drained away again.

My grandmother judged young mothers like Patricia as lost, wayward women, saying, "You see? This is what happens when you don't have God as your Lord."

That evening, Patricia came over to chat with my grandmother. I hid in bed, straining my ears to hear their conversation, heart pounding. Patricia took her time getting to the point; they discussed her pregnancy, the weather, and how badly my grandmother's laundry side-business was doing. Patricia patiently waited for my grandmother to start talking about how tight money was and then pounced.

I will always admire Patricia's tact and intelligence that night. At just eighteen years old, she was careful to distinguish her situation from other young mothers in the neighborhood, and then discreetly proceeded to say she had an idea about how my grandmother could make extra money. Soon my grandmother was eating out of her hand. To seal the deal, she casually mentioned that by doing her job for a month, I'd make the same money I would selling one hundred rugs. My ears burned. Unable to contain myself any longer, I burst into the room, blurting out how I wanted nothing more than for my grandmother to please, please, *please* say yes.

After an agonizing silence, my grandmother said, addressing Patricia only, "Don't make me regret this. The last thing I need is for this child to give me trouble like her mother did." With these soul-cutting words, she turned and walked to the kitchen to make dinner.

Still, I couldn't help nearly exploding with excitement. I didn't dare express it for fear that I'd ruin my luck, though.

Patricia and I shared a secret smile. She had done it! Because of her, I had a real shot at making something of my life. No one had ever gone out of their way to help me like that before. All the rest, I had to figure out myself. My grandmother was supportive, but being illiterate, she knew very little about the new world I was entering.

We had to find a school where I could complete seventh grade at night, apply for my *carteira de trabalho*—working card—so I could become a registered worker, and I had to learn what to wear from Patricia because my wardrobe didn't exactly spell "professional."

Everything happened so fast. Before I knew it, I tumbled along into a new routine. From nine to five, I'd work and then wait for the bus in the sweltering heat. I'd do school until 10:30 p.m., but the bus home took anywhere from ten to thirty minutes to come, so I'd arrive home at 11:30 p.m., bone tired and desperate for a cool shower and good night's sleep. The next day, I'd start all over again at 7 a.m.

After my first week of work, I tried hard not to show how pleased I felt, lest my grandmother change her mind and shatter my new reality. Life had convinced me that enjoying myself could be dangerous and to guard against hoping for too much. That weekend, I cleaned the entire house, did the laundry, and went to church three times. My performance was spotless. I knew it was stupid to expect even a flicker of praise from my grandmother, but truthfully, I never stopped yearning for even a little sign to show she was proud of me.

Of course, she said nothing.

Time flew by. My boss seemed happy with my work, and the money I made flowed through our household, filling all the little gaps. I didn't stop dreaming.

In life, there is always a path. There is always a way forward, always a way out. Dreams are roads; they allow you to imagine the steps that exist between where you are now and where you *could* be.

The morning I finally left, I found my grandmother outside, watering the plants in the yard where the concrete was still wet with soapy laundry water. I didn't dare speak to her, but in my heart, I sent a secret message. *I'm leaving this place. I'm leaving and I'm never coming back. You're wrong about me because I WILL make something of myself.* I shook as I silently delivered these words, imagining she could somehow feel my invisible determination. But she didn't even turn to look at me.

"I'm going to work, Grandma!" I said out loud.

"Go with God," she said, still not looking at me. I should explain that in Brazil, this expression can have a double meaning. With my grandmother's tone of voice that morning, though, the meaning was clear, and it's a little like an expression used here in America: "Don't let the door hit you on the way out."

I turned and left.

At the bus station, my fear began to eat me alive. It was me and my little suitcase, carrying one change of clothes, a hairbrush, and a few dollars. I tried to conceal how much my hands were sweating. How long would it be before the driver demanded to know where my parents were? My entire plan would fall apart if I didn't get on that bus, so I tried to disappear into the line and linger around a few adults who could pass for my parents. As I stepped toward the bus driver collecting the tickets, I knew everything depended on me looking calm and composed.

"This trip is nine hours long. I hope you've had a nap!" I said breezily.

He laughed. "I wish! The roads are in bad condition, though, so put your seatbelt on," he replied, taking my ticket. Just like that, I was in. I was in! It was happening. I was on my way to São Paulo, the largest city in Brazil.

SO, WHAT DO YOU WANT?

Today, I look back with compassion at both my fear and determination. Although I looked like a troubled runaway on the path of evil, I was really a spirited young woman following through with her plans and ambitions. That drive was my salvation, which was the one thing that kept me sane and strong in a life that had hurt for as long as I could remember.

Were my childhood dreams just foolish fantasies? In a way, yes. But without them, I wouldn't have been able to endure my situation. Without a vision of something better, *I would still be there today.*

Nearly everyone thinks that dreaming is somehow the opposite of concrete action. In my experience, though, dreaming is the very thing that allows and inspires action. It takes courage to dream. What if things don't work out? What if someone judges you? Trust me, I know how paralyzing fear can be.

If you have one of those "crazy" dreams inside you, give it space and time, and nurture it. See where it goes. Protect it from the world and keep it alive because it matters! Today, I have a life I am proud of. I first saw that life as a child, alone in bed, late at night with nothing to console me but my conviction that something better was possible.

Being clear about what you want is such a beautiful thing. In my life, clarity has always felt like *light*. Amid chaos, confusion, and pain, knowing what you want can provide a clarity that feels like energizing sunshine illuminating the road ahead.

I recently read the 2021 autobiography of musician, actor, and producer, Will Smith, *Will*. Granted, on the surface, I don't have much in common with him, but as I read his story, something in it spoke to me. Smith's reputation has been recently tarnished because of his much-publicized outburst at the Oscars. To my mind, however, the fact that he makes mistakes only emphasizes his humanity. His life has been messy and controversial, but it doesn't change the fact that it is also a life that has been guided by a clear, deeply felt dream.

Smith spoke about his close friend and early collaborator, JL, asking him, "What's the dream anyway? What are we trying to build here? What do we *want*?" Smith just wanted to not be broke, but he did have a yearning, even though he had shied away from it, certain that he didn't deserve to dream that big.

Mom once laid out about fifty photos of me and my brothers and sisters all throughout our childhood. She stood smugly over them and asked me if I noticed anything. I scoured the pictures like a detective trying to discover the clue that would break the case. "I don't notice anything, Mom," I said. "Look at your brother and sisters. Notice how in some pictures they're looking off to the side, or their faces are twisted, or hidden behind someone. Now look at you. There is not a single photo where you are not looking directly into the camera." I've always had a sense of the camera. I love performing. I like the camera, and more important, it likes me.

Smith's inner compass always pointed in the same direction. When JL asked him that all-important question, for the first time he was able to speak his true desire out loud. In a moment that echoes the stories of so many successful people I've met, he immediately answered JL: "I want to be the biggest movie star in the world."

JL smiled and said, "Now *that's* a goal."

In telling my story, I've tried to show the power of having a dream, communicating it to others, and allowing that clarity to guide you. I use the word "dream" a lot, but I'm not talking about an idle fantasy here; I'm talking about a clear, strong vision of what you want most in your life. Stephen Covey, the author of *The 7 Habits of Highly Effective People,* says there are only two problems in life:

1. Knowing what you want and not knowing how to get it
2. Not knowing what you want

So, how do we find out what it is we truly, deeply want? Well, like in both Will Smith's story and my own, it all starts with a question.

THE STORY OF ANTWAN JACKSON

In my volunteer work with US veterans, I encounter all sorts of fascinating people who are negotiating big life transitions. This is how I met my coaching client, Antwan Jackson (not his real name), who agreed to sit down in a one-to-one interview with me.

Antwan is a thirty-one-year-old African American grandchild of 1920s sharecroppers. His grandparents came from a long lineage of indentured servitude and were denied education. They were followed by a generation that was essentially lost to drugs, disenfranchisement, and the intentional destabilization of black urban communities. That lost generation was the generation that raised Antwan.

The entire family was deeply entrenched in organized crime, drug abuse, and violence from the beginning. His father was disconnected emotionally and seldom employed, while his mother had an addiction of her own: work. Everyone hustled. Whether it was processing kilos of cocaine or a little weed here and there, the family did what they could to make money. With the exception of Antwan and his sister, everyone in the family had been to prison.

His earliest memories were of family members cooking up batches of crack in the kitchen while he watched Saturday morning cartoons in the living room. He remembers coming back from school one day and seeing his mom loading the AK-47 on the couch in a blind panic, asking if anyone had followed him home. Antwan can even dimly remember his first coke high at just five years old.

Nevertheless, he explains his childhood was also filled with love, with grandmothers and aunts doing everything they could to hold the family together and build a sense of community. Things may have been hard at times, but there was always someone who would happily give their last, offer up a safe haven, or just be a shoulder to cry on, night or day.

Growing up, Antwan experienced learning difficulties and struggled within the confines of the classroom environment. Though he doesn't feel like he was physically abused, his mom and dad fought constantly—fistfights, throwing things. It wasn't unusual to hear gunshots ringing out in the neighborhood, either. Violence was everywhere. As kids, Antwan and his siblings would often play fight or just straight-up fight. It was their way of learning to navigate a violent and hostile world.

One day, Antwan was involved in some serious riots at school. A fight had gotten so badly out of control that soon dozens of kids were brawling and an external police SWAT team was called in, helicopters in tow. Later, conflict mediators came to the school and Antwan found himself talking to a counselor.

"Where do you think your life is going?" the counselor asked. Antwan shrugged. He didn't see himself living past twenty-five. "But let's imagine you *did* live past twenty-five. What would you want to do?"

It was a question he'd never been asked before.

Without thinking, he answered that he wanted to make movies, be a storyteller, and travel the world. This was the first time he'd ever verbalized this secret wish. For Antwan, TV had been a means of escape for as long as he could remember. He would tune out his fighting parents, focus intently on the screen, and be transported somewhere else.

Sadly, the dream was put on the shelf and life had to be dealt with. By the age of sixteen, he was on his own making $1,000 a week by dealing mostly weed, a little cocaine, and pills. But after a frightening brush with the Drug Enforcement Administration (DEA), Antwan had a new plan. He connected with a shady Mexican gang and ran a bold idea by them: With the gang's help, Antwan and his friends would threaten to burn down local stores unless the owners paid up every month. As an adult, Antwan can now see the unconscious root of this scheme: He hated what alcohol had done to his mother, and he hated the stores that sold that alcohol, not just to her but to his entire community. He wanted to destroy them.

Well, wisdom can sometimes come from unexpected places. One of the harder and more grizzled drug veterans pulled him aside and said, "What you're talking about could get you twenty years to life. Is that really what you want? Look, the streets are always going to be here, but your life, your youth… well, that won't last forever. Do something else. Join the military or something. Do that for four years and if you come back, then we'll talk."

As it is for so many people, joining the military was a turning point for Antwan. At the time, he was being sought by the DEA, and there were more than a few people in his neighborhood who wanted him dead, so what did he have to lose? The way the recruiters put it to him sealed the deal: If you're killed at war, your family gets money. If you survive, you'll get money for school. Here, at least Antwan's lifelong death wish was worth something.

Antwan never went back to the Mexican gangster. He joined the US Marines, and today calls it his "last ditch effort to reach for something not yet imagined." Today, Antwan is a respected storyteller and filmmaker who has indeed traveled the world, just like he said he wanted to.

Despite his learning disability, he graduated with a fine arts degree from an Ivy League school. Like many African Americans, he is keenly aware that his upbringing is one most people won't understand. The legacies set in place generations ago are still echoing down through a body that has endured trauma and a heart that has known the pain of deprivation.

Yet Antwan is more interested in what he has to be grateful for, and he feels privileged to have amassed so many vastly different life experiences. He can now value his unique and authentic perspective and bring it to his filmmaking, redeeming old narratives of hardship through storytelling.

Antwan is a hard man to pin down. If you ask him for advice, he won't give it. He says instead to simply *keep on asking questions*. Getting clear on the life you want starts with a question, but it doesn't end there. Keep dreaming.

Questions are valuable, but their value is not in how fast you can rush to find the answer, but in their power to keep you in open curiosity, receptive to something new.

DON'T KEEP YOUR DREAMS A SECRET

Human beings *need* dreams and goals.

Yet so many of us hide our aspirations in the dark, neglect them, and then wonder why we lack clarity. In fact, none of my coaching clients today lack the discipline or strength needed to achieve what they want. What is their only problem? The vision itself is poorly defined, if it's acknowledged at all. Reconnecting people to what energizes them most is where I come in!

If you feel lost or uninspired, I'm here to tell you your dreams are still there waiting for you. It can seem impossible to keep a dream from your youth alive. But as it lies dormant, so too does your sense of power, purpose, and clarity. I know your dreams are hidden inside you like a secret power station, just like mine were for me. I say "hidden" because there are usually a few layers of excuses piled on top.

Brazilian author, Paulo Coelho, of the bestseller *The Alchemist*, wrote an article on his personal blog called "The Three Symptoms of Killing Our Dreams." Coelho complained that a lack of time is a sign you've unconsciously abandoned your dreams. "There's no time" is just an excuse we cling to when we're afraid of taking the leap into a fuller life, one guided by purpose and joy. The saddest thing in the world is to peacefully allow your dreams to die inside you, calling it "mature" or "realistic," convinced you have no right to ask anything grander of yourself or of the universe.

Dream small, and your world will be small.

You might ask, "Who am I to dream such a thing?" But who are you *not* to dream such a thing?

Once you are reconnected to that inner compass, don't keep quiet about it. Lives can change in those moments when we speak up and share the most authentic yearnings of our heart. I get it, sharing these tender dreams with others can leave you feeling vulnerable. It's never comfortable to expose what is half-formed and tentative to the possible judgment of others.

Do it anyway. When you speak out loud about what you want in life, that vision becomes more real. The mere act of speaking aloud gives a desire shape and definition. The easiest way to deal with naysayers is to remember that they don't have any legitimate authority when it comes to what's important to *you*—unless you give them that authority. Sharing only *feels* like a risk, but in reality, most people respond well to passion and honesty.

Here's a secret. When we share our heart's true calling, others feel inspired to respond on that same level. Yes, people may judge you. But what other lucky chain of events could be set in motion because you verbalized your desires? Who are you to say what amazing role other people could play in transforming your life? None of this can happen if you don't put those desires out there first.

As I reflect on my own life, I can see that many of the goals and dreams I set for myself were achieved as a direct result of me clearly verbalizing what I wanted for myself.

THE POWER OF VISUALIZATION

Sharing your ambitions with others is important, but to what extent have you acknowledged them within yourself?

Visualization is not just some fluffy mindfulness exercise that goes nowhere. Instead, a vivid vision is the *prototype* for your future. Even the most audacious goals had to take their first baby steps in the mind's eye. Your imagination is the arena in which your fledgling dreams start to unfold their wings. The greater the initial clarity, the more powerfully they can launch.

Since the publication of *The Secret* by Rhonda Byrne in 2006, the idea of using the "law of attraction" to manifest your desires has become commonplace. But in my experience, it needs to be followed up with a key ingredient: the law of *action*. Achieving the life you want is not magic. What we create becomes real via our actions and decisions. Those actions and decisions put dreams into motion and make them a reality.

Yes, you need hard work to travel the road, but the first task is to imagine the journey.

If you're the kind of person who views things like vision boards and visualization with skepticism, rest assured that mental imagery practice is *not* about indulging fantasy or passively hoping for better days. Research by Ranganathan and colleagues in *Neuropsychologia* in 2004, discovered that simply imagining the movement of muscles resulted in real-world gains in muscle strength. This means that visualization is not just a psychological exercise that makes you feel good, it literally changes the world you live in!

The mind genuinely does not know the difference between imagination and reality. When you visualize, your brain perceives the vision as here and now, and it starts to view the world accordingly.

Lindsey Vonn was called "America's Best Woman Skier Ever" by *Sports Illustrated,* and has said, "I always visualize the run before I do it. By the time I get to the start gate, I've run that race a hundred times already in my head, picturing how I'll take the turns" (Loder, 2014). Michael Jordan uses visualization, too: "Whenever I was working out and got tired and figured I ought to stop, I'd close my eyes and see that list in the locker room without my name on it, and that usually got me going again" (*Michael Jordan: The Life*, 2015).

Visualization is not mere wishful thinking; it helps you create your new reality, one new neural connection at a time.

TAKE ACTION: HOW TO TAP INTO WHAT YOU WANT

You don't need anything special to do this exercise. After all, I did it when I was just a young girl, alone in my bed at night.

Simply close your eyes and take your time envisioning the future you want, which could include a new relationship, success in business, or good health. Weave that vision together in your mind's eye. Imagine you are a painter creating a rich and detailed world. Who are you with? What are you saying and doing? Most importantly, how do you feel? Be bold!

Look around your vision and flesh out every tiny detail. Feel the pride of holding your finished creation in your hands. Look at the dazzling view from a window in your new home. See yourself giving someone your new business card printed with your dream job title. Once you've immersed yourself as deeply as you can in this vision, keep revisiting it and keep walking toward your future.

Some people take it further and write out plans, descriptions, scenes, ideas, and even potential dialogues. You may find you want to keep a visual reminder of your dream some place where you can see it every day. Whatever you do, allow your excitement and sense of possibility to guide you. Keep tapping into the emotion of possibility and new beginnings, and welcome what emerges in you without judgment or fear.

Now, people often tell me they have trouble even getting started with this exercise. What do they want? They have no clue. If you're stuck, your deepest desires may have spent a long time underground and may just need a little coaxing to come out.

Try asking yourself the following questions to loosen things up:
- If money was no object, what would you want in your life? What would you be doing? Ignore your analytical mind when it jumps in and says, "Yes but…"

- Imagine yourself five to ten years from now. Where do you see yourself? Who are you with? How do you feel?
- What was your first dream for yourself when you were young?

THE BIG IDEA

The decision is yours: One choice is to stay in your safe comfort zone and keep dreaming small, never to know the fulfilment of bringing your vision to life. The other choice is to take the courageous step onto the path that will lead you to growth and take responsibility for what you truly and sincerely want for your life.

Dreams are not a luxury; they are a necessity. *Don't keep them a secret.* Ask honestly what you are yearning for deepest in your heart, then refuse to hide that yearning away. Instead of blaming others or complaining about a lack of time, tune into your inner compass and start creating the life you really want.

Visualization is a powerful way to clarify your vision in your mind's eye, and it helps you access focus and energy. You can use that energy to bring your vision to life through action. If there was absolutely nothing stopping you right now and you weren't afraid, what kind of life would you want to be living?

Let the excitement you feel in answering that question guide you.

CHAPTER 2

SET A GOAL

"Setting goals is the first step to turning the invisible into the visible."

—TONY ROBBINS

In the last chapter, I asked you to dream big. If nothing was impossible and nothing was stopping you, what would you really, truly want for yourself? Now, that's a useful question to ask, but it's only the beginning.

Having asked you to get excited about your heart's truest yearnings, I'm now going to put a speed bump in the road. You see, it's not enough to have a dream and then set to work on a plan to achieve it. Yes, you need a dream, and you need to work hard to make that dream happen, but somewhere between those two tasks is a crucial step many people skip over: setting appropriate, realistic goals.

Many of my clients have no trouble dreaming. For them, that's the easy part. Somehow, though, the excitement and energy the dream generates doesn't quite translate to completed action. Why? My theory is because they're missing a goal to smoothly bridge the gap between invisible and visible, between "could be" and "is."

When it comes to building the life you want for yourself, dreams are necessary, but they are not sufficient. What's more, having a dream alone doesn't entitle you to it, nor does it bring you any closer to achieving it. Unless you somehow convert that big dream into something pragmatic, realistic, and concrete, a dream is all it will ever be.

A DREAM IS NOT A GOAL

"Goals are dreams with work boots on."

—DAVE RAMSEY

Too many people are confused about the process of dreaming, goal setting, and planning. They focus on just one and assume they've addressed all three, but they're seldom successful. To create the life you want, you need all three:
1. Crystal clear *dreams*
2. Realistic *goals*
3. Detailed *plans* to achieve those goals

Without clear dreams, goals won't speak to your deepest values, and plans will lead to places you don't necessarily want to go. Without realistic goals, grand and exciting visions that propel you into action will promptly fizzle out when the real-world kicks in. Without detailed planning, dreams and goals are somehow always provisional, always somewhere far off over the horizon, and never real.

Many coaches are great at getting people excited about their dreams, but that's where it stops. Likewise, some coaches are brilliant at getting people to identify goals and fine-tune their plans, but without ever asking about the bigger purpose those plans are serving. You need all three!

Knowing what you want is like rocket fuel, but setting a goal and a plan to get there is like having a vehicle to put that fuel into and knowing exactly where that vehicle is taking you.

However, not all goals are created equal.

WHY YOU NEED A WRITTEN GOAL

Have you heard of the famous Harvard Business study that claims that less than 3 percent of Americans write down their goals and just 1 percent regularly review those goals? For a time, even prestigious publications like *Forbes* also repeated the claim that "the 3 percent of graduates from their MBA who had their goals written down, ended up earning ten times as much as the other 97 percent put together, just ten years after graduation" (Acton, 2017).

Impressive, huh? Yes, and, in fact, complete fiction. It turns out that the Harvard Business goal study is nothing more than an urban myth, although an astonishingly persistent one. Curiously enough, the results of this "study" inspired scientists at Dominican University in California to test out the hypothesis for real. Psychologist Dr. Gail Matthews and her team took 149 participants and broke them into five groups:
- **Group one** thought about their goals
- **Group two** wrote their goals down

- **Group three** wrote their goals down and also formulated "action commitments"
- **Group four** wrote goals down, formulated "action commitments," and also shared goals with a friend
- **Group five** did all of the above, but also checked in with that friend once a week

The researchers followed the groups to see how well they did with their goals. What were the results? Groups two through five were better at achieving their goals than group one, with group five performing the best of all. According to the researchers, "This study provided empirical evidence for the effectiveness of three coaching tools: *accountability, commitment and writing down one's goals*" (Gardner & Albee, 2015).

So, the so-called Harvard Business study may have been bogus, but the general claim is sound: Goals that are written down are superior to goals that are just thought about.

As I've tried to understand exactly why written goals work so well for my own clients, I've also encountered what neuroscientists call the "generation effect." This is the phenomenon where people seem to have better recall of information that they themselves write down than for material other people have written. This is why teachers recommend students paraphrase and create their own notes in preparation for an exam. By simply writing things down, the ideas become more real, more accessible, and easier to remember (Jacoby, 1978).

A written goal helps you *focus*. When you put pen to paper, you're forced to be clear about what you're actually trying to achieve. It's a filter that cuts down on vague-but-nice-sounding potentials, and whittles things down to real, achievable outcomes with a definite size and shape. Written goals help you make the transition to action, letting you see the next step forward. What's more, a written goal is like a marker you put down, which you can revisit in the future to appraise how far you've come.

For as long as I can remember, I've had countless notebooks and journals in which I've written down my goals. I'm proud to say that many ideas that existed as mere paper and ink a few years ago have now become real for me. Written goals matter, but I don't think there is anything magical about the act of writing itself. What matters is that writing down goals encourages you to be *realistic*.

HAVE THE COURAGE TO BE REALISTIC

"Everything is permissible, but not everything is beneficial."
—1 CORINTHIANS 10:23

Imagine that a dream is gigantic in size, outrageously exciting and inspiring, and as limitless as the ocean. Then imagine that a goal is like a funnel placed beneath that ocean, carefully siphoning off only a thin, focused stream of that glorious energy. Everything is possible. Any chosen goal is doable if you decide you want it badly enough. However, that doesn't mean that *everything* is doable. You are not immortal, and you don't have infinite resources; therefore, you need to be selective.

When I say people need the courage to be realistic with their goals, I am not saying their goals should be small. What I'm saying is that they need to be focused. We need to funnel that ocean down into something real and workable. A goal allows us to take the enormous potential of our dream and narrow it down into something that will work practically in the world we actually live in. We're not clipping the wings of our dreams or cutting them down to size; we're just asking, *what shape do you have to take to become real right now?* That's a big difference!

No dream is impossible to achieve. I mean that! However, a dream may be unfeasible because you simply don't have enough time available to do what's necessary, or you may have another dream that takes priority. The goal-setting process is where you sit down with your dreams and take a good, honest look at them. All of it is possible, but which parts are most feasible?

FORGET SMART GOALS

In my line of work, you encounter "SMART" goals all over the place.

The idea is that a goal is more likely to be met if it follows the acronym SMART, which stands for specific, measurable, attainable, realistic, and timely. SMART goals were first developed in a 1981 issue of *Management Review* by George Doran, James Cunningham, and Arthur Miller. Today, SMART goals are a coaching and consulting staple. Nevertheless, I think it's time to look at more effective alternatives.

Earlier in my career, I set my fair share of SMART goals, but the truth is that many of these goals never quite "made it." Why?

The goals I was setting for myself were, simply put, too shallow. I wanted to make big, sweeping changes to my life, and though the SMART framework was useful, it just did not go far enough. It told me nothing of *how* I was going to reach my goals and put zero focus on the deeper reasons I was aiming for them in the first place. There was very little room for ambitious personal development, especially in the longer term. To be frank, although these goals may have been smart, they were also small.

Let me share a few effective goal-setting alternatives that I've since discovered.

PACT GOALS

This allows you to switch your focus from outcome to process. You not only look at where you're going, but how you're going to get there.

PACT stands for purposeful, actionable, continuous, and trackable. A 2021 article by Tammy Salmon-Stephens for the *National Society of Leadership and Success* outlined each of these components:

Purposeful

Your goals need to be connected to your bigger, overarching life purpose and not just your fleeting desire in the present. If a goal isn't aligned with your broader values and overarching vision for your life, it will be much harder to commit to the goal in earnest.

Actionable

Again, be realistic. "Actionable" means you *do* something. However, don't shape your goal around what happens to you or what other people do, shape it around what is entirely under your control. Avoid getting trapped in hypotheticals, analyses, and "research." Sometimes, the best way to test an idea is to put it out into the world and see what happens.

Continuous

Your actions should be repeatable. Later in the book, we'll look at the power of habits. For now, consider that continuous improvement is more valuable than quantum leaps and overnight transformations.

Trackable

This replaces the old model's "measurable." Measuring can be useful, but it may lead to over analysis. Instead, simply ask one question: Did I achieve the action I set out to? Yes or no?

To create effective PACT goals, you need to identify something that is fully aligned with your purpose and act toward that goal with those things that are most under your control. Then, do it again. Keep going, and don't forget to ask, "is this working?"

This is simple! I love how straightforward this process is and how swiftly it allows me to take that massive ocean of a dream and focus it down into something that will genuinely make a difference in my life.

BIG, HAIRY, AUDACIOUS GOALS

PACT goals certainly helped me make simple, straightforward goals, but I still felt like some X factor was missing. When I first read about "Big, Hairy, Audacious Goals," or BHAG, I realized exactly what that X factor was: size!

Originally developed by Jim Collins and Jerry Porras in their 1994 bestseller *Built to Last: Successful Habits of Visionary Companies*, Collins claimed, "The power of the BHAG is that it gets you out of thinking too small. A great BHAG changes the time frame and simultaneously creates a sense of urgency."

What I love about BHAG is that they're for the long term. These are not just five- or ten-year plans we're talking about. These are *life* plans.

President Kennedy wanted to go to the moon. Google wanted to collect and organize nothing less than the sum of humankind's knowledge. Microsoft didn't just want to sell computers but put computers into the homes of every person on the planet. It's important to note that all three of these goals were once considered outrageously ambitious. Today, just a few decades later, we take them as given.

BHAGs are most commonly seen on the corporate or organizational level, but I believe everyone should have their own personal BHAGs, too. Your goal should be:

Big—*Really* big. Something that takes more than a decade to achieve.

Hairy—Your goal needs to challenge you. Is it a bit crazy and "out there"? Good!

Audacious—You know what audacious means by the way it makes you feel. Is it a goal that gets your heart racing? Does it make you sit up and pay attention?

I like to combine both PACT and BHAG. When using PACT and considering goals that speak to your purpose, aim high and think of your purpose in the biggest, hairiest, and most audacious terms possible.

Be careful, though. BHAGs require some honest soul-searching. These goals must *genuinely* feel compelling and exciting. For example, if the thought of being the world's best in any endeavor leaves you cold, don't feel that you have to aim for that to do your dream justice.

Once you've identified your big dream and visualized it clearly, pass it through a funnel until you're left with a workable, realistic goal. Dream big, then work small. Set your sites as far as you can, then put your head down to ask what you can do, day by day, to get there. Bearing in mind the dreams you identified in the previous chapters, ask:
- What single goal, if I achieved it right now, would have the biggest impact on my overall quality of life?
- What is the smallest, simplest repeatable action I can take *today* to bring me closer to that goal?
- How can I keep track of my process as I go?

The best goals are about moderation; they're just the right size, neither too small nor too big. They push the envelope, but they're also not unrealistic. They speak to the values you and only you hold for your life, but they also challenge you. We honor our dreams when we take them seriously, but also when we expect them to stand up to the demands of real life.

This leads me to one important final consideration: Sometimes the best thing to do with a dream is to decide not to pursue it.

LETTING GO OF A DREAM

Many of us are forfeiting our potential because we don't allow ourselves to dream big or because we dream big and let that dream lie dormant within us. We hold ourselves back in life because we don't honor our dreams with goals to match.

Sometimes, though, what might be holding us back is the dream itself. This is a dream that has outlived its purpose.

Many years after I left Brazil, and once I'd been living in America for some time, I remember visiting Boston and encountering the statue of John Harvard. As I watched tourists eagerly posing their children in front of it for photos, I was told about the prestige and legacy surrounding this man and the university he helped found.

Like me, the tourists were dreamers. Yet as I looked at their happy, hopeful faces, I was filled with an unexpected sadness. Why are some people lucky enough to be born into loving families? Why are their lives blessed with all the resources they'll ever need to plant them firmly in a successful future that they'll never doubt their entitlement to? Why wasn't I one of them?

In that moment, a small dream took root in me. I sat on the Harvard yard lawns, and for a moment, I imagined I was one of them. I imagined I was one of the lucky ones.

Years later, I was working at Goldman Sachs and BlackRock, two of the powerhouse firms on Wall Street. There, being able to carve out my path to vice president of investments without a scrap of formal education already felt like winning the lottery. When you work at companies like that, though, you're frequently surrounded by impressive leaders and colleagues with degrees from Yale, Stanford… and Harvard. For me, these people were figures of enviable stature. Could I be that educated, happy, and confident?

I decided I too would get a formal education. Not just any formal education, but a degree from Harvard. They would say, "Oh that's Paula, she went to Harvard." I didn't care if I had to wait until I was in my seventies to start working on that degree. I would get it, and I would prove to myself and everyone that I was capable.

Now, I want to be clear: This Harvard dream was real for me. I meant it 100 percent. Yet after working on myself for years and healing old wounds of shame and self-doubt, I gradually realized I no longer needed it anymore. My Harvard dream was born at a time in my life when I craved external confirmation of my own worth. One day, I realized I had achieved more personally and financially than many of the people who had gone to Ivy League schools. I no longer needed an institution to validate my self-worth because I had faith in my own ability to learn.

I've now retired my Harvard dream, not because I doubt whether I can achieve it, but because I no longer need to (here's a hint: You can always unretire a dream later if you want to!). The dream was always "permissible," but it was no longer "beneficial." When I realized this, I finally admitted to myself how I'd been holding onto this dream out of some misguided sense that I owed it to my former self.

In my work as a coach, I often see adults clinging to dreams they planted in their hearts when they were teenagers. Maybe the dream was planted by somebody else. They feel like they're betraying themselves by letting go of these dreams. You can look at it another way: By releasing these dreams that no longer serve you, there is more space in your heart and mind for new possibilities.

Values evolve. Dreams evolve. As we grow and mature, so too does our vision of our best possible life, and that's a good thing. Give yourself permission to retire ambitions that are no longer important. What we want and need when we're young changes, so don't feel forced to hold yourself loyal to a childhood goal that no longer resonates.

You haven't failed! You've just grown and so have your dreams.

THE BIG IDEA

The decision is yours: One choice is to leave your deepest dreams unexamined, unspoken, and unfulfilled, and live a small life lacking clarity and energy. The other choice is to do the difficult work of dreaming big and challenging yourself to set goals that will actually get you there. I know it's not an easy choice, but it is a choice you have.

Dream big, but remember that when it comes to creating the life you want, dreams are necessary but not sufficient. Start with crystal clear dreams, then funnel them into more focused, realistic goals, which then allow you to plan. This allows you to act.

Not all goals are created equal. Accountability and commitment are important, but the most effective way to make your goals mean something is to *write them down*. This will keep you focused and motivated.

Everything is permissible, but not everything is beneficial. Be selective about where your time and energy go, and choose goals that are feasible in your world. Use the PACT acronym to create goals that speak to your *p*assion, are concretely *a*ctionable, *c*ontinuous, and *t*rackable. Also ask yourself if your goals are BHAGs—big, hairy, audacious goals. Dream big and challenge yourself to go for the long-term goal that truly excites you.

Not everything makes it through the funnel. You evolve and so do your dreams, so don't get stuck trying to fulfill a vision you've long outgrown.

CHAPTER 3

HAVE A PLAN

———

"If you don't design your own life plan, chances are you'll fall into someone else's plan. And guess what they have planned for you? Not much."

—JIM ROHN

ZIGZAGS

A dream was deeply engraved into my heart and soul: I would go to America. So why was I now on a plane, making my way to Italy?

Let me explain.

When I first arrived in São Paulo, I was fifteen years old, and my most urgent mission was simply to find work. Once the thrill of having left home wore off, I focused myself on the task of earning money. I found work as a receptionist and rented a bed in someone's house. Piece by piece, I built a little life for myself.

For as long as I could remember, I had been telling people about my dream of going to America. This explains why I was a little confused when one day—while working at my second job at a clothing store—a coworker said, "You know Paula, you're always talking about going there, but why don't you go to Italy?" I blinked. It wasn't something I'd ever considered. She continued, "You can't go to America 'cause you don't have a visa, right? But you don't need a visa to go to Italy."

But what about America?

I knew from an early age that I had only two choices in life: I could keep daydreaming about something better, or I could start *doing* something about it. So I created a crystal-clear vision, and I dedicated myself to making it a reality, no matter what. I knew exactly what I wanted and that was a life completely different from the one my grandmother predicted for me—a life in America.

Yet no sooner had I set myself on that road did I face my first obstacle: There was just no way I could get a visa to even step foot in the country. I'd always known I would need a plan, but this was the first time my plan was tested. That day, something inside me shifted, and I realized that simply having a goal is no guarantee you will travel smoothly from A to B.

The path to success is never linear. No direct highway will take you from where you are to where you want to be. You may need to travel some bumpy, potholed backroads, and you may find yourself on routes that are not exactly scenic. The truth is that things often don't go according to plan, and we need to reassess the situation, adjust, and proceed.

Don't let a long and winding path discourage you!

At first, going to Italy felt like a wrong turn. I knew I'd be lonely there, and I would have to overcome massive language barriers. But my friend was right; if getting a visa to America was a problem, I'd just have to find a way to move forward without one. So, I went to Italy.

I'll be honest, it was never my intention to live there. Still, I was excited because Italy represented one step further away from the life I wanted to leave behind and one step closer to the life I yearned for.

In Rome, I found odd jobs walking rich people's dogs, cleaning their houses, and watching their kids. Even though the path had seemingly taken a diversion, I hadn't for a second forgotten the ultimate destination. I continued to tell anyone and everyone about going to America, and I still kept scanning, ears pricked, for whatever opportunity would take me closer to it.

Sometimes, lucky breaks and life-changing opportunities enter your life, but they are in disguise.

One day, I met a couple who asked me to watch their son for a few hours on the weekends. The husband was Italian and a professor at a university in Rome, and the wife was American, also a professor, who taught Italian literature at Dartmouth College. What was an unremarkable nanny job on the surface turned out to be a major pivotal moment in my life mission. The couple invited me to come with them to America, offering to pay for my airfare and provide me housing. In exchange, I'd live there, look after their son, and keep the wife company.

Who would have thought my journey to America needed to first pass through a country on the other side of the world, more than five thousand miles away? It wasn't all that long until I was on a plane, feeling the bump of the wheels touching down on the runway at Logan International Airport in Boston. It was surreal. All those countless nights spent imagining this exact moment and all those childhood dreams of one day making my way to the country in which I'd build my perfect life *was finally happening.*

Nothing can describe my joy at that moment. I watched my long-held dream materialize in front of me, and it was exactly as I had imagined it.

What I hadn't imagined, though, was the zigzagging path it had taken to get there.

YOU NEED A PLAN

Just because life takes unexpected turns, it doesn't mean you don't need a plan. In fact, it's proof of how much you *do* need one.

If you ask people what they'd like to achieve in their lives, their answers will vary. People will talk about their desire to lose weight, ramp up their careers, make more money, learn a skill, or create a happy, beautiful family life. However, if you ask the same people if they've developed a specific plan to achieve these goals, you'll get a depressingly uniform answer: no.

Having desires and dreams is easy. However, few of us have actually written down a specific plan to achieve them. Without a plan, we are all at the whims of life's random zigzags, chance, or other people's intentions for our lives. I can tell you that what you want for your life is not going to spontaneously fall into your lap this way.

I never once let go of my dream of going to America, and that vision became like a lighthouse, constantly reminding me of the direction in which I needed to orient myself. Without that lighthouse calling me, I would have gotten distracted and lost in Italy. But on the other hand, plans need to be flexible enough to accommodate the unexpected. If I had been too rigid about how my plan was "supposed" to play out, I never would have gone to Italy in the first place.

Life is messy and hard, and as I learned in Italy, sometimes the only way forward is to take an elaborate sideways detour. Dead ends, challenges, and mistakes are not obstacles in the path, they are the path. However, with a plan, you create a sense of order and calm on that path, even if you're surrounded by chaos or the unexpected.

WHAT IS YOUR *BIG WHY*?

When most people think about planning, they think the process is about writing down a list of action steps or making a to-do list. Granted, that's an important thing to do, but in my experience, it's not the best place to start when it comes to creating a plan that works. After all, if I had approached my own journey this way, I might have still been stuck trying to answer the question, "How am I going to get to America?"

Instead, I believe one of the most effective ways to begin a life plan is not to start with a list of steps but to begin by asking yourself the right questions.

When you ask (and answer) powerful questions, you tap into your deepest motivations. These are the dreams and goals you identified in chapter 1. Your *Big Why* is the lighthouse. If you can see it on the horizon, you can confidently navigate any obstacle in your way. Without it, you have no idea where you're going.

On his blog, Tony Robbins claims that, "Quality questions create a quality life. Successful people ask better questions, and as a result, they get better answers" (2021). We could blindly follow a list of steps for a process we believe we should commit to, but it's far more powerful when we allow the right questions to guide us instead. Trust me, when plans emerge from deep self-knowledge of what really matters to us, they are bulletproof and unstoppable.

"How am I going to get to America?"

This question made sense on the surface, but the trouble was that it was narrow enough to shut out the path that would eventually lead me to the outcome I was looking for. So instead, I asked myself:
- *"What do I need to do to get myself out of here?"*
- *"Where could I go to increase my chances of success?"*
- *"If this isn't working, what will?"*

I needed to open my perception and come up with alternative routes to get to where I wanted to go. To do that, I needed more than a generic action plan or list of tasks that didn't speak to my *Big Why*.

Let me tell you the story of Marty Cooper, a young engineer at Motorola who was given a new assignment in the 1970s. His job was to head a team that was tasked with developing the next generation of "car radiotelephone." However, Marty didn't leap in with a plan that consisted of a list of tasks. Instead, he paused and got curious. He asked himself a question that shaped his thinking from that moment on: "Why is it that when we want to call a *person*, we have to call a *place*?" (Shiels, Economist, 2009).

It's a question that seems almost too simple, but its power came from how it questioned everything that was currently taken for granted. Digging deep down into the problem they were actually trying to solve, Marty was able to gain insight into a new path of innovation. They would sever this connection between person and place, and make it so a person could be reached no matter where they were.

By 1973, Marty would be the force behind the DynaTAC 8000X, or what he affectionately called "the brick." This cellphone prototype had an abysmal battery life of less than half an hour and cost $4,000, but it was the device that ushered in a new era of communication and earned Cooper the accolade of "father of the mobile phone." It was a path that would not have unfolded without Cooper's initial question (Shiels, Economist, 2009).

Asking questions is not just for inventors and innovators looking to solve a problem. If we want to grow and evolve in our lives, we too are faced with a problem: How are we going to get ourselves from where we are to where we want to be?

KIMBERLY NEELY'S BIG QUESTION

Kimberly Neely is a larger-than-life Detroit woman who had to do precisely this. We sat down together, and I asked her to tell me about her life and how certain challenges forced her to ask the kind of questions that would cut to the core of what she actually wanted for herself.

Her story starts back in 1960s Motown, where she was raised as the third of nine siblings. Her childhood was a raucous one filled with big, colorful personalities, parents who both used and sold drugs, and a carousel of people coming into the house, including people the kids called "junkie flunkies." Kimberly had to learn to find sense in a world of complete chaos and uncertainty. With her two eldest siblings tangled up in drugs, Kimberly took on the role of the eldest child. This role didn't last long because at the age of fourteen, Kimberly became pregnant.

When the baby was born, there was an instant connection, one that would shape her mindset for the rest of her life. From that moment on, Kimberly vowed that everything would be for her daughter; she called her Angel.

For years, Kimberly scraped by on part-time jobs, government assistance, and plenty of hustle. By the time she was in her early twenties, she'd accumulated more life experience than many people ten years her senior.

Today, everyone knows about affirmations and personal mantras, but Kimberly was doing it long before it was popular. She recalls how, in the midst of panic, she'd go quiet inside and say to herself, "Calm down. You're not the first person to go through this. Other people have been here, and some have survived. Some haven't. So just think—what did the people who survived do? Well, do that."

Kimberly's *Big Why* was to build a good life for herself and her daughter. Instead of asking how she was going to secure this or that apartment or how she was going to bluff her way into this or that job, she asked herself deeper questions.

One of the things I love most about Kimberly's story is how razor sharp these questions were, and how she leveraged them to create a plan that kept her calm, clear, and focused. "What do the people who survive do? Well, do that." And she did.

Today, Kimberly is a life coach helping other people find their own source of strength and purpose. She's not only earned her bachelor's degree but also her master's degree, and she has built an incredible life for herself and her daughter. Kimberly's path has certainly had a few twists and turns, just like mine did.

To me, she is a master of inspired action and an expert at using questions to drive concrete, practical plans.

START WITH A QUESTION

Plans matter, and the most effective plans are those that are born from asking the right questions. Questions are not only catalysts for creating something new or finding novel solutions, they're also milestones on the road to help you keep on track. Questions can help you uncover your values and principles and shine a light on what is and isn't working. I am so passionate about questions that I have a collection of them that I often return to, in my own life and with my clients:

1. What is the one goal that would have the greatest impact on my life?
2. Why is this my goal? What is my *Big Why*? Why is this goal important?
3. Who do I need to become to achieve my goal?
4. What will I lose if I don't follow the plan? What will I gain?
5. What one action can I take today to move me a step closer to my goal?

Write everything down. Be honest with yourself, and don't be afraid to ask questions about your process, either. Pause and ask, "Is what I'm doing moving me forward?" or "Am I asking the right questions?"

The best plans I've ever put in place started with me asking questions. Even as a child, I had the dream to escape the place I grew up, and I constantly asked, "Where do I need to go? How can I get there?" The questions themselves weren't magic, but through them *inspired action* was possible, and it was this that propelled me out of the place I was and toward the place I knew in my heart I wanted to be.

HOW TO MAKE A PLAN

"A goal without a plan is just a wish"

—ANTOINE DE SAINT-EXUPÉRY

Planning is not just important, it's nonnegotiable. Our lives today are built on the choices we made yesterday. Are we going to make sure those choices are working to bring about the future we want? I've always believed you should dream big. However, when you sit down to make a plan to reach that dream, you set to work refining it, shaping it, and yes, sometimes, cutting it down to size. When you plan, you give yourself the gift of exploring whether a path is realistic and genuinely achievable *before* you embark on that journey.

Not everything is achievable, and not all goals are appropriate, but planning helps you identify the ones that are. You can plan a route that will make the very most of it.

If you have a plan, you break everything down into smaller, more manageable chunks. Instead of getting overwhelmed as you gaze out at how far you still have to go, you put your head down and focus only on the next step you need to take. When big goals seem vast and unconquerable, a plan brings everything down to earth, tells you to calm down, and allows you to look at the practical tasks in front of you.

If you can embrace planning in this way, you boost confidence in your abilities. Every small step you take is proof that you can solve problems and advance. You may encounter obstacles (correction—you *will* encounter obstacles), but if you are armed with a plan, you can have faith in your competence.

Every goal comes with a cost, and every path to that goal has hazards along the way. If you have a rock-solid plan guided by the right questions, you manage your risk in an intelligent way, rather than just blindly reacting to problems.

Making plans can seem intimidating, but I assure you that investing this time in yourself will more than pay off in the long run; the process isn't complicated. Ray Dalio, founder of the world's largest hedge fund Bridgewater Associates, is considered one of the world's greatest investors. In my mind, Dalio is a champion heavyweight in the field of achieving the life you want. In his 2017 book *Principles: Life and Work,* Dalio claims that success is a healthy mix of three things:

1. Clearly identified dreams
2. The willingness to embrace and deal with reality, as it is
3. The determination and hard work to realize those dreams, given reality

According to Dalio, our task is to build the future we want for ourselves in the world as we find it, and for this, we need a plan and enough hard work to see it through. His observation has always been that successful people are able to dream big while still accepting reality for what it is (Matthew Lekushoff, 2021).

A plan is a strategic way to bridge *what is* with *what could be.* Successful people don't complain or wish things were different. They readily accept the playing field as it is, and they find smart ways to navigate through it so that they achieve what they want to achieve. In his book, Dalio proposed a simple five-step process for success, but with my own coaching clients, I work with a similar but expanded nine-step process:

1. **Decide what you want:** As you did in chapter 1, imagine you could wave a wand and your life would be perfect. What would that look like for your family, your career, your finances, and your lifestyle? Identify your *Big Why* and the ambitions it inspires.

2. **Write it down:** Imagine you are ordering your deepest desires from a dream factory. Be as specific, clear, and detailed as possible.

3. **Set the timer:** "One day" means never. Set a deadline for yourself, and, if necessary, break that down into smaller, more manageable deadlines.

4. **Know what you're up against:** Why haven't you achieved this goal already? Identify what's standing in your way (hint, it's usually you) and find a path around it.

5. **Tool up:** Identify and seek out the information, resources, ideas, and tools you'll need to achieve your goal. What *one* skill will most help you get there? Focus on that.

6. **Choose your team:** Establish a support network by identifying the people who can help you achieve your dream.

7. **Make a list:** Write down every action you'll need to take to achieve what you want. A journey of a thousand miles starts with a single step. What is that first step?

8. **Make a plan:** Organize all these tasks into a coherent, step-by-step plan—down to the month, week, and day.

9. **Set priorities:** Zoom in and identify that single most important task for each day to focus on. What is the best use of your time?

Most of us have been taught to jump in at around step seven or eight, without properly considering our goals, our values, the resources at our disposal, or the potential drawbacks waiting to undermine our efforts. If we allow questions to guide us, however, both our goals and the plans we set to achieve them are kicked up to the next level.

Ask anyone who's achieved success and they won't say they arrived there by accident. They won't say they excelled by following a standard script borrowed from someone else's life, either!

DON'T FORGET TO PLAN WHAT YOU *WON'T* DO

"If you have more than three priorities, then you have none."

—JIM COLLINS

Let's look at that final point in the process: "set priorities." Planning is about turning that laser focus onto what you want, but it's also about everything that you choose *not* to focus on. What do you really want? In answering that question, you can't help but choose between alternatives. In other words, anything is possible, but not *everything* is possible.

Sometimes, it's tempting to get sidetracked by a lot of relatively insignificant details, but beware because every ounce of energy you spend on distractions is an ounce of energy that doesn't go toward what matters. When you spread your attention across many different goals, your plan becomes like a diffuse beam of light—scattered and weak. When you focus that attention on just one important goal, it becomes as bright and powerful as a laser.

When you plan, try to practice discernment and be selective with where you invest your attention and what you will consciously ignore. Here again, the right questions can help you find clarity:

- Are there any minor goals you are spending too much time on?
- Are there any major goals you are allowing yourself to neglect?
- If you are honest, which goals are actually a waste of your time?

The difference between major and minor goals is simple. Major goals are the ones that would have the *greatest* impact on your life if you were to achieve them. Minor goals help, but they're not the heavy lifters. Ask yourself: If you dropped a certain goal, would it ultimately matter to the bigger picture? If not, it's just a minor goal, not a major one.

By answering these kinds of questions, you're less likely to get derailed or distracted. You'll find it easier to set up boundaries and say no to things that don't ultimately align with your priorities. Every time you say *yes*, there is also something you are saying *no* to. Choose wisely!

THE IMPORTANCE OF HAVING A FINANCIAL PLAN
Time is not the only thing we need to learn to budget. We also have finite amounts of energy, willpower, and, most importantly, *money*.

I have found both in my past corporate career and now in my work as a coach that what stops a person from achieving their goals is often a lack of financial confidence. Some lack the belief that they have the resources needed to support their goals. Others have the financial resources, but they don't have the confidence to use them strategically. Sometimes people are taken aback when I start talking about financial planning in a discussion about life goals. They may think, "but my goal isn't even about finances."

I couldn't disagree more. Putting sound financial plans in place is important for everyone, whatever your goals are. Without a financial plan, you cannot create, grow, and protect the financial resources that are likely needed to reach your goals.

I know money isn't everything, but whether your goal directly involves finances or not, experience has taught me that all goals we set for ourselves have a financial component. As a consultant of investments for top financial advisors, I've heard all sorts of finance horror stories. My husband is Randy Doroff, CEO of Fathom Advisors (yes, I believe in the value of having a financial advisor so much that I married one), and he has heard all the same stories.

I have personally seen families destroyed because there was no safety net in place for when disaster struck, be it in the form of unexpected terminal illness, job loss, or the death of the primary breadwinner. Some of these stories are desperately sad, and some have happy endings. Perhaps my work has made me biased, but from my perspective, the difference between them is simply a sound financial plan.

Glynne Bassi is a successful financial advisor with Edward Jones in Minneapolis, but not that long ago, she was thirty-four years old, divorced, jobless, and had three young children to care for. She was more than one thousand miles away from family, and she was financially clueless. She didn't even know her bank account numbers or passwords. Though difficult, this crisis taught her just how important financial planning is. Today, Glynne's life purpose is to educate and empower others to feel confident in their financial future so they don't have to go through what she did.

Many people think of financial planning as a boring chore, but it's anything but. Britt Williams Baker is a money coach and co-founder of Dow Janes, and she teaches women to strengthen their relationship with money and remove the obstacles holding them back from creating the lives they want. While chatting with her about the power of financial planning, she told me:

> *The way that I see it, the importance of money and having a financial plan is so you can have freedom. Freedom of choice. Freedom of who you spend time with and how you spend it. Basically, freedom over what you do with your life. Whether that's saving enough to retire or saving enough that you can earn passive income from your investments—it's all much easier if you have a plan.*
>
> *Unfortunately, not enough of us are taught this in school or by our parents. So people don't learn this until they're in their thirties or forties, and by then they've gotten used to a lifestyle that actually doesn't*

*allow them to save money or create freedom. I want
everyone to be living their best life, to be doing the
work that they're passionate about and to be spending
their lives the way they want to. When money is taken
care of, when money isn't something that keeps people
up at night, basically, anything becomes possible.*

However, when it comes to having a financial plan, most
Americans just don't think about it. The 2015 National Financial Capability Study discovered just how few people prior-
itize financial planning. They found that 75 percent of baby
boomers, 87 percent of millennials, and 81 percent of Gen
Xers have no written financial or retirement plan. Just 18
percent of people had written plans in place. Here are a few
more staggering statistics:

- 42.3 percent of Americans have less than $10,000 saved
  for retirement (GoBankingRates survey)
- According to the Federal Reserve, American savings
  accounts have a median balance of $7,000, and 39 per-
  cent of Americans would struggle to cover an unexpected
  $400 bill
- The National Endowment to Financial Education claims
  that less than a quarter of millennials have basic financial
  literacy

Many people think that professional financial guidance is
a luxury. Yet in my line of work, I have witnessed firsthand
how expensive it is to *not* have a financial strategy.

Some people lack confidence, feeling that the process is too
complicated, overwhelming, or stressful. But here, research
tells us the opposite is true: The 2021 Schwab Modern Wealth

Survey found that 65 percent of people who claimed to have a written financial plan felt financially stable and secure, whereas for those who lacked a plan, only 40 percent felt this kind of comfort. What this tells us is that financial planning *reduces* stress and worry and increases self-confidence. When you're working with known quantities, you will inevitably feel more in control and able to manage uncertainty.

THE BIG IDEA

"Failing to plan is planning to fail."

—ALAN LAKEIN

The decision is yours: One choice is to forego making concrete and realistic plans, and then see where random events or other people's actions take you. The other choice is to take matters into your own hands and start creating plans that will get things done, regardless of the obstacles you may face.

The path to your dreams can take unexpected turns, but a good plan will help you stay the course. It's not enough to simply make a list of tasks. We need to start with a question, and let this inspire us toward a plan that makes sense.

Decide what you want, write it down, set a deadline, identify obstacles, tool up with the resources required to overcome those obstacles, get a support team, and *then* make a list that puts your tasks in order. It's also important to decide what you won't do, such as identify your priorities and keep your focus on them and not on distractions.

Finally, have a realistic financial plan to fund your vision, whatever it is. Don't allow a lack of confidence to deter you. Proactive financial planning and embracing *what is* will boost your confidence and reduce the stress of the unknown.

Look to establish a relationship with an experienced financial advisor and take that relationship as seriously as the one you have with your doctor. If you already have a financial advisor, don't be afraid to get a second opinion. Your financial well-being is too important for you to accept mediocre service and advice.

CHAPTER 4

GET COMMITTED

———

"Unless a commitment is made there are only promises and hopes, but no plans."

—PETER DRUCKER

THE TEST

They say God tests us.

For me, that test's name was the "Series 7 Security Licenses." It was unlike anything I'd done before, and at 125 questions and almost four hours to tackle them, it was considered one of the most difficult securities licensing exams out there. The test allowed people to officially join the securities industry in the United States as a general securities representative and assessed their mastery of things like stocks, bonds, and investment risk. In short, it's like the security industry's version of the bar exam.

I worked at a calling center for American Express Financial Advisors in Minneapolis as an internal consultant. My job was taking calls from financial advisors and answering their questions about mutual funds and annuities. I had been in the United States for just under three years, and I'd never taken a formal English class. The English competency I did possess had been gleaned from a few workbooks I'd found and the daily interactions with the people around me.

My obvious accent embarrassed me at times, and I often found English expressions incomprehensible, but I pushed on. Half the time when someone was explaining something to me, I'd smile and nod, hoping they couldn't tell I had no idea what they were saying. I'd always felt insecure about my lack of education, but now I also felt insecure about my inability to express myself. Behind the nodding and smiling was the constant, desperate thought, *do they think I'm an idiot?* If only they knew.

In this job, all it would take was for me to give a financial advisor incorrect information, which means I'd end up costing everyone money. Or even worse, I'd cause an advisor to do something that was not in compliance. My career could come to a screeching halt, no question.

One day, my boss, Mary Jo, called me in for a meeting.

"Paula, you're doing a good job, and I want you to know that. Everyone has told me how focused you've been with learning as much as you can, and everyone loves how positive you are." I smiled and wondered what was coming. "The head of our department is saying that we need to make sure that everyone working on the phones has their securities license and most of the sales consultants are already licensed. In your case, you're not, so that's something we need you to start working on right away."

I was like a deer in headlights. The Securities and Exchange Commission (SEC) had been coming down hard on anyone who either provided any type of financial advice directly to consumers or advised those who then gave that advice to consumers. "The license is the one that financial advisors need to get to be in the business of giving financial advice. You learn about investment risk, taxation, equity, debt instruments, packaged securities, options, retirement plans… it's administered by the Financial Industry Regulatory Authority, which is overseen by the SEC. The exam will be scheduled for the next couple of weeks, since Dan is giving everyone ninety days to pass. It's not easy, so the sooner you start the better. Does that make sense?"

Make *sense*? There was that familiar feeling in the pit of my stomach. Only ninety days? I panicked. The writing was on the wall: pass this test or lose my job. All I wanted was to make Mary Jo proud and prove to her that she had made the right decision when she took a chance and hired me.

Later, I learned of a few financial advisor candidates who wanted to join the company but were turned away because they couldn't pass the Series 7. They were Americans and college educated; if *they* couldn't pass, how on earth was I going to? I was already struggling to keep my head above water just learning about the job and now this. People wished me luck, but I wondered if everyone secretly thought I would fail. I couldn't think straight for the rest of the day.

The study materials were massive books, and they were as thick as the Bible. I sighed and told myself, "Just take it one page at a time." At the back of my mind, though, was something darker. *"If you fail this test, Paula, you'll lose your job, and you'll be right back in your grandmother's house, and you'll have embarrassed everyone who took a chance on you. Everyone who thought you were stupid? Well, they'd be right."*

Word by word, sentence by sentence, I picked my way through those books, usually with a dictionary by my side. I'd need to master it all, *and* carry on learning the ropes at work, *and* perform flawlessly in my role. As you can imagine, the weeks that followed were some of the most intensely stressful weeks of my life.

A page that took some people two minutes to read took me twenty minutes. I woke at 4 a.m., crammed in a few hours of study, went to work, studied during lunch, went home, studied late into the night, and did it all over again the next day, with extra on weekends. I even had nightmares that I was back in Brazil again, dressed in tatty clothes and rubber flip-flops, with my grandmother plunging that old dagger into my heart again and again, "See? You *did* end up an embarrassment to the family!"

At work, people tried to gently lower my expectations and prepare me for the worst. They told me not to burn myself out and that many people didn't pass the first time. In fact, about 35 percent of people fail! Unsurprisingly, this made me feel worse but even more determined to get it done. I refused to listen to people who sowed doubt in my mind.

For many days while I was studying, I would burst into tears and a deep terror would wash over me. Yet even in my exhaustion, I prayed for God's help and, inspired by a co-worker who'd been talking about visualizing your goals, I vividly imagined my computer screen and the words: *Congratulations! You passed the exam!* Slowly, the anxiety would leave me and be replaced by waves of happiness, pride, and relief. Just like I had as a child, I clung to that vision as I fell asleep, like a drowning person clinging to a raft.

That vision came true.

I achieved 87 percent on a notoriously difficult exam on complicated material that was new to me, in a language I had been speaking for less than three years, while working. I had a middle school education from a third-world country (which I'd kept secret), full-blown imposter syndrome, and a mountain of shame and anxiety to grapple with, *but I had done it.*

That day, I strode into the office on a cloud. I was *not* stupid. I was capable of great things, and now, since I wasn't studying anymore, I had a load of free time and energy. What was I going to do with it?

Some others who had passed the exam took a half day off to celebrate, but there was only one thing I wanted to do—*work.* I was determined to learn as much as possible, be the best I could, and make up for everything I lacked. Work was the only thing I could bet on.

ARE YOU COMMITTED OR JUST INVOLVED?

With a bacon and egg breakfast, what's the difference between the chicken and the pig? Well, the chicken is involved, but the pig is really *committed!*

I like this joke because it clearly highlights that merely putting energy into an endeavor is not the same as being committed to it. In today's world, we are all encouraged to be consumers and to go out and pick and choose what suits us and abandon it as soon as it doesn't. We are not a culture that understands commitment. We latch onto goals and work hard at them, but only if it suits us. When excitement wanes, we move on, looking for the next high.

Let me tell you my opinion on inspiration: it's worthless.

The Gallup poll found that "with only 21% of employees engaged at work and 33% of employees thriving in their overall wellbeing, most would say that they don't find their work meaningful, don't think their lives are going well or don't feel hopeful about their future" (Gallup, 2022). *Fortune* magazine (Leonhardt, 2022) cites the US Bureau of Labor Statistics' alarming reports of 4.5 million Americans quitting in 2021.

Granted, this massive shift in the employment landscape has many complex causes. People have had to grapple with home schooling, remote working challenges, and the continuing fallout from the pandemic. I know that for many people, resigning has nothing to do with a lack of commitment to work, but more with the fact that commitments to other priorities have taken precedence. Any way you look at it, crisis tends to shine a light on where your commitments really lie. A change in conditions is enough to make the *majority* of people abandon their employment and seek a situation elsewhere. What does this tell us?

Well, articles talk about people's flagging "motivation." People are no longer eager or inspired enough to carry on, they say. And therein lies the problem: If we are basing our actions on how excited we feel, we are doomed from the start. Making our fleeting desire and interest a condition for hard work means we quit when motivation wanes or something more interesting crosses our path.

To make a long story short, it's a crisis of commitment.

Committed action takes motivation and desire out of the equation. We act because action is how we build the outcome we want, and that's all. We are not *required* to be passionate, inspired, or motivated in order to act. It's not necessary for it to be easy. All that's necessary is that we act.

Committed action differs from uncommitted action in that it always takes place, *no matter what.*

It's easy to be passionate and inspired when you imagine the amazing end result. But what about when you're in the thick of it and you are faced with millions of difficult, uncomfortable, and boring steps to get through? Well, if passion and inspiration were all you had to power you, you'd give up.

Inspiration and passion will get you started with a bang, but commitment is the only thing that will keep you going long after that initial thrill and buzz wear off (believe me, they will wear off). Luckily, you don't *have to* continue to be excited by the grand goal. You just have to commit to it every day. Commit to the very next action that brings you closer. Then do it again tomorrow and again the following day.

Why does any of this work? *Why* bother working hard and being responsible? As Holocaust survivor and psychiatrist Viktor Frankl famously said, "He who has a WHY to live can bear almost any HOW." The source of lasting commitment to action is your core motivation and deeper underlying reason for doing things. If you do not act from your deepest core motivation or that motivation is not noble or enduring enough, it will abandon you when the tedium of hard work sets in. Your *Big Why* means you say, "I'm committed to making this work" and not just, "I'm willing to make this work… as long as it's easy to do so and costs me nothing."

Again, it's the difference between being involved and being committed. Ask yourself: Are you merely working on a goal because you're currently inspired by it and because it's easy and fun? Or are you committed to keeping up the hard work once all of that inspiration burns off?

THE MEANING OF HARD WORK

"When you work for someone, make sure that every night when you go to bed and your head hits that pillow, you know you gave so much that day that your boss *owes you money*." I laughed the first time my grandmother, Maria, told me this. Your effort should exceed your compensation? Really? But she was right. My life has been proof that if you do that, God will do the rest. My grandmother's advice meant that at every job I worked, my bosses always told me I was their hardest working employee.

I knew from the get-go that the odds were against me, but one thing I did have going for me was that hard work never frightened me but excited me. That's why, in a way, starting with nothing can be the biggest blessing in disguise because it teaches you early on that there are no shortcuts to lasting success. Many people wish they were more intelligent, more talented, or just luckier because they think these things make success easier to achieve. Wanting to find the easiest path through, however, is precisely the opposite of the attitude you need for success.

One of my favorite quotes from Jim Rohn is, "Don't wish it were easier. Wish you were better."

My grandmother's words of advice may sound shocking to some, especially in a world where many people are dedicated to getting as much as they can, while giving as little as possible. No matter which way you cut it, there's simply no substitute for hard work. Maria Bartiromo says, "Don't ever, ever, believe anyone who tells you that you can just get by, by doing the easiest thing possible. Because there's always somebody behind you who really wants to do what you're doing. And they're going to work harder than you if you're not working hard (Brainyquote, 2022)."

Ask yourself honestly how hard you are working on your own goals. A great goal is not enough, it needs your effort to mean something. I have no quick fix or cheat code to offer; if you want success, you're going to have to work hard for it. Getting organized is hard. Setting goals and making plans is hard. Pushing through resistance is hard. Acting is hard. No matter how brilliant and dazzling your goal is, it will always come with a hefty portion of slog! Though hard work may raise you up slowly, you are *sure* to rise. If you wait for a miracle or lucky break, you could be waiting a long time.

Think of the people the world admires and you will find that they all possess an unwavering commitment to keep working hard *no matter what.* There is no inspirational hero who is ambivalent, lazy, or uninterested. It's a contradiction in terms.

Nelson Mandela created a mammoth legacy as an international peacemaker, leader, and first democratically elected president of South Africa. Mandela was a political prisoner for a whopping twenty-seven years. He was released from prison at age seventy-one—an age at which most people would consider any monumental achievement an impossibility. But according to him, "It always seems impossible, until it is done." Mandela wasn't lukewarm about his convictions. He didn't fight Apartheid every once in a while when the mood struck him. Instead, he was committed. He looked at the task ahead of him, grasped it, and refused to stop working until he made a difference.

Oprah Winfrey speaks about being inspired by Mandela. The school she opened for girls in South Africa was not some generic project, it was something she brought her whole heart into making a reality. She told *The Huffington Post,*

> *For me, the journey to open The Oprah Winfrey Leadership Academy for Girls was one of the most challenging and ultimately rewarding I've ever experienced. This was something I felt I had been growing toward my entire life. [...] People have no idea of my tenacity.*

Once I commit to something and I have a full-hearted desire to see it work, I can't imagine what it would take to make me quit.

This rings true to me; you want it so that the possibility of *not* working hard on your goal is not even something you consider. You look at obstacles and say, "Okay, I see you. But I'm going right through you."

TAKE RESPONSIBILITY

"99 percent of all failures come from people who have a habit of making excuses."

—GEORGE WASHINGTON CARVER

Are you over twenty-one? If you are, you're an adult who is responsible for your life! If you're not taking responsibility for your life, what's stopping you? Sometimes, the answer is an unconscious expectation that someone else will do it for you.

When we have response-ability, we are able to *respond* to the facts and demands of the world we find ourselves in. Being responsible means being able to accurately see your role in the creation of your life.

Like Antwan realized, you can blame your childhood, you can whine about injustice, and you can point the finger at others, but at the end of the day, you only have two choices: you can choose to accept responsibility for your own life, or you can forfeit it and push that responsibility onto other people or things. However, when you avoid responsibility, you also give up control.

We do not have control over other people—what they think or what they do. We do not have control over certain events or circumstances of life. We do not have control over luck or chance. We only have control over ourselves.

So why would you give up the only control you *do* have?

People think being responsible means you take on the burden of things that are not in your control. You may think that "you're responsible" means "you're to blame!" This is an immature idea of what responsibility is. When we are responsible, we take firm control of what we can: ourselves. We take responsibility even if it's difficult or scary, and even if we're not quite sure of what we're doing and make mistakes along the way.

Responsibility means you claim your own personal power, and nobody can claim it for you. When you accept your accountability, you put yourself in the driver's seat. You give yourself the chance to choose, and from then on, every choice creates your life the way you want it to be. You are proactive and not just reactive.

If we don't acknowledge and claim our responsibility, we are never truly making choices. Instead, we give that power to others and let them choose and act for us. We submit to circumstance. Sometimes it's more convenient to *blame* the person in charge than *be* the person in charge, right?

I mention responsibility because it's what makes the difference between commitment and merely being involved.

Responsible people have had a deep realization: If they want something to happen, they're going to have to do it themselves. Nobody is coming to *give* it to them. When we forfeit responsibility, we shrug and say, "Well, my success at this goal is not up to me. It's not my job. Somebody or something else is in charge, and it's not me."

Responsibility, commitment, and hard work all go together.

If you don't acknowledge your responsibility to change a situation, how can you ever commit to making those changes? And if you don't commit to a goal, how are you going to do the hard work that's required?

Nothing is more common in this world than people who are ready to make everything someone else's fault. It's easy to find a million "reasons" for why you can't improve your situation—there's no time, there's no money, you had rotten parents, the system is working against you, you don't have the talent, people are being difficult, it's hard, and so on.

Look closely, though, and these are garden variety excuses. Every time you make an excuse, you're denying yourself the gift of your own power. That may be easy and comfortable for a while, but I can guarantee you, it's not the path to success and inner fulfillment.

I know being in control is scary, but it's also a powerful place to be.

HARD WORK IS A QUESTION OF HABIT

*"Sow a thought, reap an action; sow an action, reap a habit;
sow a habit, reap a character; sow a character, reap a destiny."*

—STEPHEN COVEY

Here's a question: Did you brush your teeth this morning?
Chances are, you did. You probably brush your teeth every
morning and have done so since you were a child. This
action takes practically no effort because it's automated. It's
so ingrained that you probably feel weird when you *don't*
brush your teeth. You once had to learn how to do it, but
now, you barely even think about it.

That sense of *automatic habit* is what keeps us working hard,
consistently. A habit has a special kind of magic in that it can
make the right thing the automatic thing. Action matters; not
just a single action, but many actions, repeatedly. The way to
cultivate committed hard work is to *focus on process rather
than outcome.* A goal can feel like it's somehow outside of
normal life, and once we achieve it, normal life will continue
as it did before. But a habit is different. It's not just part of
your life, it is your life.

Imagine if every day you worked toward your goal with
the same regularity that you bring to brushing your teeth.
Habits are small things that, when compounded, create epic
outcomes. Some habits take thirty days to become ingrained,
others take longer. Once a habit is automatic, you open a
whole world of continuous improvement. The fantastic thing
is you already have habits. Why not make the habits you

have work for you and the life you want to create? Consider the following example.

Person A has a *goal* to lose ten pounds.

Person B has a *habit* of never eating second helpings.

Person A may have some success on a crash diet, but the habit Person B forms could last a lifetime, not to mention it will make other healthy habits more likely. Person A may be overwhelmed at the size of the task and give up at the first temptation, but Person B isn't looking that far ahead. All they have to do is avoid having seconds today and that's it.

Fast forward a year and Person A has long since abandoned their lofty goal. Person B is still diligently and consistently avoiding second helpings, easily and automatically. Eventually, it becomes so much a part of their life, they barely even notice it anymore. They lose ten pounds as a matter of course and keep it off.

Habits are what commitment looks like when it's out walking in the real world. You must have a dream, set a goal, make a plan, and then commit to that plan. Don't commit just once, though. Commit each and every day so that working hard becomes nothing more for you than a simple, everyday routine. In my work as a career and life coach, I have never seen a goal achieved in any other way.

HOW COMMITTED ARE YOU?

Once you've identified a dream and made a goal and a plan to reach it, it's time to get real about your level of commitment.

- On a scale of one to ten, with ten being "I couldn't be more committed," what is your level of commitment to your goals right now?
- Are you committed or merely involved?
- Are you willing to increase your level of commitment? If the answer is yes, how do you imagine yourself doing it?

Let's return to the pig and the chicken because I want to suggest a little twist to the tale. You see, the pig gets slaughtered to make bacon. It doesn't want to be killed, no doubt, and losing its life this way is something that can only happen once and never again. People think of commitment and hard work this way—as something that burns you out or kills you completely.

What about the chicken? The chicken lays an egg every day. It lays eggs because it's a chicken, and that's what it does. It couldn't stop laying if it tried, and a healthy chicken will lay useful eggs for years. In a way, this sustained and consistent effort over time looks more like my vision of commitment.

We can turn the joke on its head and say the chicken is most committed after all. Because to me, commitment isn't something grand and sacrificial we do just once. Instead, it's the ability to give your best, day in and day out, sometimes for years. It's something that becomes a part of our life, a part of who we are. Working hard at our goals should feel as natural and nonnegotiable as a chicken laying an egg every day!

THE BIG IDEA

The decision is yours: One choice is to relinquish your responsibility, make excuses, and wait around in vain for someone to give you the life you want on a platter. The other choice is to commit to the goals you care about and understand that the only way to bring them to life is with sustained, genuine effort.

Once you've identified what you really want for your life, set your goals, and created an intelligent plan to reach those goals, you need one crucial ingredient: hard work. There is never any replacement for hard work. We cannot do the hard work required, however, if we are merely *involved* and not truly *committed*. This means consistent, day-to-day commitment like the chicken, not once-off martyrdom like the pig!

We need to commit to our goals, and be honest enough to give up on the excuses holding us back from owning our choices and taking responsibility for our lives.

We don't achieve our goals overnight, but we can achieve them step-by-step, day by day. It may not be glamorous, but consistency and habit are the secret. People think you need to be inspired to commit, but experience has shown me it's the other way around: Commitment brings inspiration. Just take action now—even if you're unsure and even if that action is imperfect at first. Then take action again tomorrow and the next day!

"Most people fail not because of a lack of desire but because of a lack of commitment."

—VINCE LOMBARDI

CHAPTER 5

GET INVESTED

———

"Your greatness is limited only by the investments you make in yourself."

—GRANT CARDONE

The first hard truth: Nobody owes you anything, and if you want something, it's your responsibility to make it happen.

The second hard truth: There is no replacement for hard work. There is a price to pay for the things you want, and that price is hard work, every day, as a matter of habit.

The third hard truth: You cannot wait for someone to invest in you.

I would never have passed the Series 7 Securities License exam without dogged determination and commitment. But I would never have been able to commit without first understanding that it was my job, and mine alone, to build the life I wanted.

Commitment sounds like a great idea, but where does it actually come from? I've heard it said that *investment creates commitment.* Or, in more blunt terms, you need to have skin in the game. If you don't first take that leap of faith and invest in yourself, nobody else will do it for you.

WHAT DOES A DREAM COST?

"Invest in yourself to the point that it makes someone else want to invest in you."

—TONY GASKINS

Let me ask you a question: How often do you randomly invest in someone who is taking no steps toward helping themselves?

If your answer was "never," I want you to pay attention. You see, most people give precisely the same answer.

As a career and life coach, I come across way too many people who are quietly waiting for others to make things happen for them. Maybe they're holding out for their family's blessing or encouragement or waiting for their employers to pay for them to take a course or earn a certification. Sometimes they're not even sure where they expect this help to come from. Nevertheless, they feel they cannot act unless someone else believes in them first.

Would you buy the stock of a company if you knew its leadership was not investing in the future growth of that business?

A stock price is a direct correlation to its investment on growth. We need to look at ourselves in the same way.

When you wait for others to give your life direction and meaning, nothing happens. However, if you invest in yourself, you:

- Learn new things
- Get out of your comfort zone and grow as a person
- Set goals that are appropriately sized and challenging enough
- Become more qualified
- Make the best of opportunities that come your way

The degree to which you can do the above is directly proportional to the size of your growth and achievement. How much and the frequency you invest directly impacts the returns you get. That's finance 101, right? When you pay for something, you are unconsciously saying, "This has value. This matters." Words, ideas, and fantasies are cheap—in fact, they're free!—but when you put skin in the game or you "pay" a price, you deepen your commitment.

When you take ownership of your life, you don't wait for others to say, "I see value here. This is worth doing." Instead, you invest in your own goals. Whether that's energy, time, money, or some other resource, why would you wait for permission to pursue what's most important to you? Other people—leaders, bosses, and experts—are not the gatekeepers of your growth, and you don't have to wait for their approval or help to take action.

I understand some people don't have the financial resources to, for example, hire a coach. Well, as someone who literally works as a coach, I want to tell you, that shouldn't stop you! If you can't afford a financial advisor, buy a book by a financial advisor. If you can't afford the book, go online and sign up for a free course or find YouTube videos. If you can't afford the internet at home, go to the library and use theirs!

With the tools and technology available today, investing in yourself is as affordable as it's ever been. I also want to assure you that anything you can pay to learn, you can learn without paying.

ACTION LEADS TO COMMITMENT

Reluctance to self-invest sometimes comes from the faulty belief that inspiration leads to commitment.

You know how the saying goes: "If I feel energized and passionate about my goal, *then* I'll be ready to commit." But can you see the problem? You are making inspiration a condition of your action. So you sit around and wait for that mythical inspiration to hit. You wait and wait. We look at others and wonder why they aren't super enthusiastic about us or our life plans, which is silly, right?

Truly, I believe it's the other way around. Action leads to commitment.

Commitment is like a snowball, and it won't get rolling on its own. The more action you take, the more you build motivation to keep taking action, and you create momentum. But *you* need to take that first step, whether you feel inspired or not. The momentum can go in the other direction too. The less action you take, the less motivated and inspired you feel to take action in the future.

If you say, "I can't advance at work because my employer won't pay for the course I need," then recognize that this is just an excuse. Okay, your employer is not investing in you, and maybe they have no faith in you. But do *you* have that faith in yourself? It's less easy to blame others for not advancing our interests when we realize how little we've done to advance them ourselves.

Motivational speaker, Les Brown, breaks it down in his You-Tube clip better than I can. He says you have a choice: you can have *reasons* or you can have *results,* and that's it. You can point out all the reasons—excuses—that you haven't achieved greatness and why you're not living the life you want to live. Or, you can have results. You can't have both (247 Motivation, 2021).

In a way, we are always committing. We are either committing to mediocrity or committing to greatness. We commit to either making excuses or finding solutions. Too many people say "I want to do better," but they don't commit any of the time, energy, or money that's required. If you don't, who will?

Legendary personal development author Jim Rohn once said, "Work hard at your job and you can make a living. Work hard on yourself and you can make a fortune" (SUCCESS, 2017). Warren Buffett, the world's greatest investor, told *Forbes* magazine "Ultimately, there's one investment that supersedes all others: Invest in yourself." Despite having a net worth of $80 billion, he sees human potential as the ultimate value. After all, the improvement you make to yourself is something that can never be taken away from you.

Think of yourself as a precious commodity. Commit your finite and precious reserves of time and energy to their highest possible use. The next course, workshop, or certificate is great, but you need to *constantly* be learning. When you get to where you're going, set your next goal. Your boss expects a certain degree of performance from you, but that doesn't mean you can't define your own parameters, set your own standards, and identify your own limits.

Evolving is not something that happens by default. Evolving is something we must consciously choose for ourselves.

Why should you invest in yourself? Well, honestly, you don't have to. However, if you don't, nobody will care, and nobody will force you to.

If you want something bigger and better, you need to commit. You need to invest in yourself.

THE INVESTMENT OF TIME

Are you thinking that this word "invest" implies needing to spend money and lots of it? Money is just one thing we can pledge toward creating the life we want. Although people can be reluctant to spend hard-earned money on their dreams, I find there is often something they're even less willing to invest: time.

If you want to know what you are committed to in your life, look at how you spend your time.

Be honest, and ask yourself how much of your time you've committed to working on yourself. How much time have you devoted to learning new skills, reading, acquiring knowledge, or digging deeper into your values and guiding principles?

I worked for twenty years as an investment consultant to financial advisors, and I sincerely believe that the work you do on yourself is one of the few investments in life that will *always* pay off. Try not to make the mistake of thinking that just because you're "busy" that you're being effective. Some actions you take today do precisely nothing except waste time, while others you take will pay off many times over in the years to come. Be honest about which actions are filling up your days. If someone tells me they're "too busy" to invest in themselves, I'll be honest and say I don't think they have their priorities straight!

Work harder on yourself than you do on your job. What matters is *your value* because it is irreplaceable.

At least, this is the advice of Jim Rohn. Of course, I don't think this means you should slack off at work or financial and professional success isn't important. However, I do think we can get trapped in daily work routines—forgetting about the bigger picture beyond our job titles or what we earn. In fact, I think if you follow Rohn's advice and work hard on yourself, you automatically become a more valuable employee anyway.

HOLD YOURSELF ACCOUNTABLE

"Accountability breeds response-ability. Where there is no accountability, there will also be no responsibility."

— STEPHEN R. COVEY

Accountability gets us out of our heads and puts our abstract hopes and fantasies out into the world to be tested.

Success is not a million dollars in the bank, a big house, or a fancy car. Success is how well you are able to consciously design your life the way you want it. *That* is what you want to invest in. Hint: when you do, all that other stuff tends to follow.

When we take a risk and come out of our comfort zones, everything suddenly becomes real. Putting our intentions out there means one of two things can happen: failure or success. If you don't put yourself out there, only one thing happens: automatic failure. Holding yourself accountable means knowing there is no chance of success unless you can also stomach the risk of failure.

It's not just coaches like me who think accountability and investment go hand in hand. Research has shown that accountability is the secret ingredient to achieving your goals. The Association for Financial Counseling and Planning Education (AFCPE) reported on a study conducted by the Association for Talent Development. This study examined the relationship between accountability and goal achievement and found:

- People who had a goal were generally 10 percent likely to achieve it.

- People who consciously decided to achieve that goal boosted their success rates to 25 percent.
- People who specified when they'd achieve the goal reached 40 percent.
- People who made a plan to achieve their goal did so 50 percent of the time.
- People who made a commitment to someone saw the likelihood rise to 65 percent.
- And most astonishingly, a specific accountability appointment with someone you've made that commitment to means that you are 95 percent likely to complete that goal.

Read that again—that's *almost a 100 percent chance* of completing a goal!

Pearson's Law states, "When performance is measured, performance improves. When performance is measured **and reported back**, the rate of improvement accelerates" (Doug Wick, 2008). When you have a deliberate appointment set with someone, with the express intention of revisiting your commitment to them, your chances of success shoot through the roof. I hope this explains why I am such a big fan of accountability coaching!

DON'T FORGET TO CELEBRATE YOUR SUCCESS

I was so thrilled about passing my Series 7 exam that I immediately raced into the next challenge. Looking back now, I should have taken more time to pause and just acknowledge the work I'd done. When you celebrate your successes, it reinforces what works and boosts your confidence. Putting your head down to work is essential, but you also need to lift it up again once you reach a milestone, look around, and honor your progress.

Of course, I don't think you need to wait for a success as big as the Series 7 was to me back then. I believe you should celebrate even the small victories. Stanford University's Dr. BJ Fogg, author of *Tiny Habits: The Small Changes That Change Everything,* agrees, saying habits are not formed merely by repetition but by pairing each event with a positive emotion.

The actions celebrated are the actions most likely to be cemented as habits. Don't just think, "huh, good job," go all out! Throw your hands up, scream out loud, or do a little dance; whatever it takes to make you genuinely feel that rush of positive feeling. When you do, you are creating a powerful unconscious association around that behavior, making it more likely that you'll repeat it in the future.

One more reason you need to celebrate every success—big or small—on your path is because there's nothing virtuous about burning yourself out or making yourself a martyr. We live in a world that constantly pushes us to aim higher and higher. No sooner have we topped our personal best, do we take that new level of achievement as a given and start looking for the next goal to aim for. Living this way can make you lose sight of just how far you've come and miss out on many potential feelings of pride and satisfaction.

Which milestones should you celebrate? How should you celebrate them? Well, I will leave that up to you. We each decide what we count as a success, as well as what it means to us when we cross that finish line.

KEVIN BJERKE'S LEAP OF FAITH

There's no way around it, evolution *always* happens outside of your comfort zone. Take responsibility, hold yourself accountable, and celebrate your success when it happens.

Most importantly, invest in yourself!

Sometimes, you must have faith in yourself even when everyone else thinks you're a bad investment. Sometimes, you must act even if you're petrified, or you're not ready, or your confidence in your abilities is shaky at best.

This is precisely what Kevin Bjerke learned the hard way, and sometimes the hard way is the only way.

I first met Kevin when we worked together at Ameriprise Financial. Over the years, I learned more about him, and he shared his story about how he'd been abandoned by his birth mother on the streets of South Korea when he was just five years old. In the early 1970s in South Korea, being born to an unmarried, young mother carried enormous stigma and so did being born mixed race. Kevin was both. It's no surprise that he felt like the odds were stacked against him from the beginning.

Kevin grew up to be a "bad" kid. He stayed out late at night, got terrible grades, and found himself caught up in a destructive flurry of drugs, alcohol, and smoking. The anger and shame he felt, however, was only ever directed at one person: himself. Back in the 1980s, there was little understanding or compassion for the kind of childhood trauma he'd experienced and support was practically nonexistent.

Feeling aimless and adrift, he saw the teenagers around him similarly lacking structure and purpose and on paths going nowhere. Some were in jail already. Yet despite the adversity heaped against him, and despite the total absence of role models, he felt something stir inside. It was the clarity that this was not *his* path. He was meant for something different.

That's when he took his leap straight into the deep end and joined the US Marines.

It was tough. At first, he couldn't even run a mile, but this baptism by fire was exactly what he needed. Military life was his unofficial initiation rite into adulthood (the kind of thing he feels is sorely absent in the modern Western world). It taught him to cultivate responsibility, discipline, and hard work. His training took him overseas for four years, first to the first Gulf War, then to Spain, and then to a counter-narcotics operation in the Caribbean.

The deeper skill set his training provided was instilling in him a mature, structured approach for overcoming adversity, and he kept this with him long after his service ended. That mindset rested on the holy trinity of accountability, responsibility, and self-investment.

At some point in your life, you'll get a deep feeling that something needs to change completely and drastically—something big. If you're feeling lost and directionless, like Kevin, it's time to be brave and make the leap. It's time to invest in the next step.

This is the time where you most need to take a risk and act, even though you may not feel 100 percent ready. Kevin is the perfect example of how inspiration doesn't lead to committed action but vice versa. Take action and the commitment will come. For Kevin, taking the leap even when he felt unprepared was the key.

If you're feeling lost, don't ignore that voice inside asking for something better. Listen to it, and allow it to lead you. When you're afraid, it may feel safer to take tiny steps or barely dip your toes in. However, in Kevin's US Marine Corps training, he learned to ignore this resistance and push on anyway. Don't be afraid to get thrown into the deep end. After all, that's how your most intimidating fears are rechristened as your most cherished strengths.

Choose challenges where you have enough skin in the game that failure would actually mean something. For example, with my Series 7 exam, the challenge was already built in: pass or lose my job! You'd be surprised how much you can achieve when you tell yourself there simply is no road back to your old life.

Even if you do fail, so what? You need to prove you can survive. Like Kevin, teach yourself that fear is part of the deal, and there's no reason not to leap with both feet into the next phase of your evolution.

The surprising thing about Kevin is that despite his impressive success forty-five years on from those dark days in the orphanage, he doesn't actually consider himself exceptional or particularly intelligent. He'd tell anyone he was mostly average. If asked to share the principles behind his success today, he would say discipline, accountability, and total commitment win out every time. It's the art of going all in.

No matter what has happened in the past, any one of us can choose to invest in ourselves at any moment. *You don't need to be exceptional* to make an effort or to make that effort consistently. *You don't need to do it perfectly.* Kevin's life proves that genius and raw talent is nice, but commitment is what moves you from point A to point B. It's a myth that if something is truly your path and your purpose, it should be effortless.

If you feel like your life is lacking purpose, don't wait for someone else to come to save you—that's your job. Kevin might have felt like he started the race with a significant handicap, but his adversity forced him to learn one of life's most powerful lessons: We are always in control of ourselves. Hardship is not a problem. What matters is what you do with it. When you take responsibility for your experience, for your life, and for your future, you are *living on purpose.*

Today, reflecting on an illustrious career and enviable success, Kevin says something surprising. He says *he* was always his own worst obstacle. Even after finding a degree of corporate success, he was still haunted by old addiction demons and numbed away the stress of a high-powered career with alcohol and escapism. He's battled addiction to nicotine, alcohol, oxycodone, morphine, and the toughest crutch of all—sugar! He always comes back to the lessons he learned from the most challenging times of his life: You need to take responsibility for yourself.

We are not entitled to anything, and today is a gift that will not come again. None of us have infinite time here, but we can choose to focus on what matters right now. We can take responsibility, and we can choose to invest in what matters.

THE BEST INVESTMENT YOU'LL EVER MAKE

I have done my best to try to convince you of the value of investing in yourself, but I also believe that it's something that only starts to make sense when you experience it for yourself. Even the most impactful coach can't absolve you of the responsibility to take your life into your own hands!

Doug Lennick is CEO and co-founder of coaching and leadership group think2perform, and when he reviewed this very chapter, he couldn't help but add, "*Do* something. If nothing is what you want for yourself, then doing nothing is perfect. If, on the other hand, you want something for yourself, doing nothing won't work."

Read a book. Get advice. Sign up for a course, go to a conference, or find an accountability partner. Test out a combination of all of these. Maybe investing simply means taking a leap of faith and spending a little money on yourself. I don't know what will work best for you and your goals, but I do know with 100 percent certainty that if you invest from a deep sense of personal responsibility, it will pay off.

As you've probably noticed, I love asking questions, and I want to share some of the questions I introduce to coaching clients as they learn to invest in themselves:

- In what ways have you invested in yourself in the past twelve months?
- What are the top five reasons your employer should invest in you?
- What is holding you back from investing in yourself?
- What action can you take now, even though you're not 100 percent certain or ready?
- What small achievement have you already accomplished, and how can you celebrate that?

Here's an exercise: Close your eyes and imagine that a kind and generous fairy godmother has arrived to help make all your dreams come true. Imagine her waving her magic wand and granting you the thing you most need to succeed right now. Then, open your eyes, look carefully at what this thing is, and *commit to giving it to yourself*, right now. Do you need time, training, support? Invest in such a way that you give that to yourself.

In closing this chapter, I want to get personal for a moment. For those of us who have not come from privileged backgrounds, and for those who didn't always believe in their own self-worth, working on personal development can be difficult. I've known people who can work like machines and commit every last shred of effort they have to someone else, and yet never extend that same commitment to their own growth.

If you've never been valued by others, it can take courage to value yourself anyway. If you struggle to have faith in your own abilities, I know it can be scary to spend time and money and effort on something that isn't even real yet.

However, in my experience, even small moves in the right direction can yield massive returns down the line. Give yourself a vote of confidence, invest in yourself, and know that you've taken a step toward achieving your goal. I can promise you will not regret it.

THE BIG IDEA

The decision is yours: One choice is to leave your potential unfulfilled and passively wait for someone else to grant you the resources to build the life you want for yourself. The other choice is to take initiative and pour your energy into the only resource you will have from the day you are born until the day you die: yourself.

Your success is directly proportional to the amount you're willing to invest in yourself. Nobody owes you anything, and even if they did, your personal evolution is not something anyone could do on your behalf. You are your own single greatest asset, so act like it!

Take the risk of putting your goals out there and have the courage to hold yourself accountable to that vision. There is only so much we can achieve if we never take the leap and invest in what we believe in. Ask what you are waiting for others to grant you, and take the initiative to give it to yourself instead.

Don't forget to take a moment to pause and celebrate your wins. In a world that constantly pushes us to seek the next goal, it's easy to forget how far we have come and what we have achieved.

Nobody in the world is quite like you. Your life is a precious one-off that could be gone tomorrow. Think carefully about what gifts you—and *only* you—can bring to the table. Have you been doing everything you can to fulfill this potential?

CHAPTER 6

BE NICE

---

*I've learned that people will forget what you said, people will forget what you did, but people will never forget how you made them **feel**."*

—MAYA ANGELOU

"Open this."

My first professional job in America was working reception in Laramie, Wyoming. Paul Kehrer, my boss, had called me in for my annual review. I was desperately trying to hide my anxiety that morning when he slid a white envelope across the desk. I stared at it, unable to move.

"Well, open it."

"What is it?"

"Open it and you'll see." Inside was a plane ticket to Phoenix, Arizona and two $100 bills. I stared at Paul, waiting for an explanation. He smiled. "A year ago, I told you about the goals I had for my business, and how you could help me, and

Paula, you've helped me more than I can say. You've been amazing. We not only hit our goals, we exceeded them. A lot of that is thanks to you."

I couldn't remember ever receiving such a positive compliment in my life. I had no idea what to do with the warm blush spreading across my face.

"You once told me your dream was to work for a big company in a big city. I'm going to be honest, if I was being selfish, I'd keep you all to myself, but I care about you and want you to reach your goals." My mind scrambled to guess where he was going with all this.

"You see, we've qualified to attend the National Leadership Conference in Scottsdale at a resort just outside Phoenix," he continued. "I asked the corporate office for permission to send *you* to that conference as well. There will be a lot of powerful people there, including the CEO of the company. If you want to network and chase your dream, Paula, this is your chance."

I was stunned. He had arranged for another employee to cover for me for the four days I'd be away and gave me $200 to put toward new professional clothes to wear to the conference. I simply could not wrap my head around the fact that the man in front of me was going out of his way to help me achieve my dreams with no obvious benefit to himself. Was he some kind of angel God had sent to help me? This new feeling of being noticed and appreciated slowly sunk in, deep into all those secret places my childhood had long left empty.

I did go to that conference. I did meet many interesting people there. In time, I did end up working for a "big company in a big city." By the end of 1999, I was working in the American Express office in downtown Minneapolis. I wouldn't have been able to do it without the contents of that little envelope and the kindness of the man who handed it to me.

HOW HOT CHOCOLATE AND A MUFFIN CHANGED MY CAREER

I don't need to tell you that there is plenty of darkness in this world. I don't need to say how unfair, cruel, and disappointing it can be at times. Especially in business, most of our social interactions are merely transactions, and our connections to others are limited to the exchange of money, anonymous market forces, or plain old greed and fear. I want to assure you that beneath all that, there is a hidden network of kindness and humanity that is holding everything together.

Corporate America is no picnic, and the financial industry is a harsh, male-dominated world that rewards a certain cut-throat, winner-take-all mentality. Or so I thought. Later, in the job I finally found for myself working for American Express Financial Advisors in Minneapolis, I was taught firsthand about the power of kindness. Hard work matters, yes, and of course you must be tough. However, these things pale in comparison to the ability to engage people on a human level and speak to their hearts and souls.

To tell you the full story of Paul Kehrer's kindness, I need to rewind a little and tell you about how I landed the job in the first place.

It was early 1998, I was flat broke and starting over—again. My last professional job before I left São Paulo was working for a small investment consulting firm as an assistant. After months of unemployment and desperation, I opened the phone book and picked the first investment company I saw: American Express Financial Advisors. *Okay, I'll start with them.*

Although it was punishingly cold outside, I braved the snow and gale-force winds downtown to drop off my new resume, only to be greeted by a receptionist who was even colder than the ice outside. She looked at me pityingly and within a matter of seconds explained she couldn't help.

Crestfallen and close to giving up, I suddenly had an idea, and a few minutes later I was back at reception.

"What are *you* doing here again?" she asked, annoyed.

"Well, it's so cold outside, and I saw the coffee shop and thought you might appreciate a cup of hot chocolate and a muffin," I said. "I just wanted to say thank you for talking to me earlier, when I'm sure you're very busy." Heart pounding in my ears, I turned to leave before she could reply.

To my amazement, she followed me, calling out to me to stop. When I turned, her face had softened into a smile. She apologized and explained she was just having a rough day. She took my resume and promised to pass it on. The next time I heard from her, she was inviting me to meet the district manager; apparently, my persistence had impressed him.

When I first met Paul Kehrer, he was nothing like I'd expected. He told me he was originally born in Tanzania, but he went to boarding schools in England when he was thirteen and lived there for many years. He vividly remembered how hard it had been to come to this country and forge his own path. I was surprised to hear that in another life he'd spent ten years working underground in the mines.

I told him there and then that I was willing to do anything required, and I'd work as many hours as necessary. I thanked him profusely for the chance to meet him and told him I wanted him to think of me as an investment with a guaranteed return. He laughed at my audacity, but I wanted him to know more than anything that I would not disappoint someone who had given me an opportunity.

More than that, I would not waste one drop of kindness that had been shown to me.

Within a few weeks, I had the job. On my first day, the sun was shining, and the weather could not have been more different from that first snowy afternoon I had waltzed in with hot chocolate, a muffin, and a desperate hope for someone to give me a chance. My mood, too, could not have been further from the despair and hopelessness I felt that day, standing alone in the snow.

I inhaled the fresh, clean air of spring, feeling the happiest I had felt in a long time. I had a job! A real job! A job with a company that people have heard of! *American Express Financial Advisors,* I loved saying the name. At that moment, I had no idea how much more kindness Paul would show me in the years to come.

On that dark, winter day, I was ready to believe the world was a cruel and unfair place with everyone only looking out for themselves and to hell with anyone else. I thank God for the instinct I had in that moment to choose kindness instead.

The world can seem incredibly cold at times, but kindness is like a warm cup of hot chocolate. It changes everything. Keep that little moment of kindness and sweetness warm; sometimes it's all that's needed to make a connection, reach out to somebody, and remind yourself that underneath everything, we are all just human beings. Many of us have experienced the same despair and disappointment that crushed me that snowy day. And many of us have experienced the miracle of kindness in their own lives and want to pay it back.

That leads me to my third and final story of kindness.

ROBERTA AND THE MAGIC OF PAYING IT FORWARD

I know people do "favors" for one another, but few people do them without wanting something in return, right? My dear friend, Roberta, was the woman who taught me that kindness is, in fact, much, much more than this.

In the fall of 2001, while working at the American Express office in downtown Minneapolis, a woman approached me as I waited at a Dayton's Department Store salad bar for my lunch order.

"Are you from Italy? Are you Italian?"

My English at the time wasn't great, but hers was even worse. We somehow managed to communicate. "No, I'm not, but I did live in Italy, and I came to the United States from Rome. You?"

"Actually, my father was born in Italy. I'm a Brazilian Italian," she said.

"Oh wow, *I'm* from Brazil!" I said, smiling. In a mix of English and Portuguese, we struck up a conversation, and she told me her story. Her name was Roberta, and she'd fallen in love with and married a businessman who used to pass through her airline counter. She admitted that, after moving, she had no friends or family, so there and then I gave her my number and we made a pact to keep in touch.

A few months after we'd struck up a friendship, she called in a flood of tears. "My husband is telling me I need to go back to my country. He just decided that he doesn't want to be married anymore and he's going to drop me off at the airport this afternoon." I had to think calmly but quickly.

"Stay there. We're on our way." I told my fiancé, Randy—who is now my husband—this was an emergency, and we both rushed over and found her hysterically crouched by her bags in her apartment. She had almost no money, no place to go, and no survival plan. Her husband had given her a measly $300 to go back to Brazil.

After talking things through with Randy, we decided to let Roberta live with us until she figured things out. She didn't have an education or a profession. She didn't have a car. She barely spoke English. Remind you of anyone?

I was working insane hours and had a packed schedule, but I didn't care. She needed help, and I was going to be the one to give it to her. I made it my mission to do everything in my power to help her. At first, I helped her organize her driver's license and find a full-time job, but in the end, Roberta lived with us for a full six months until she was able to rent a room and slowly start a new chapter in her life.

Even after she moved out, we stayed in touch. In 2005, her mother, Mara, moved to the United States and became a close friend as well. She quickly became irreplaceable and played a significant role in all of our lives, including my two sons who soon considered her their grandmother.

I'll admit I was drawn to help Roberta because her plight reminded me so much of my own, and I'd be lying if I said helping her was not something that ultimately fulfilled *me* on a deep level. After all, Roberta's mother, Mara, gave me the kind of love I'd never received from a woman in my life before. In truth, the real gift Roberta gave me was the satisfaction and honor that comes with knowing you've made a difference to someone's life.

She's now married to a man she adores, Jeff, and has a rewarding career as a veteran's nurse in Florida. Although I credit her success to her raw strength and intelligence, I also like to think I did my part, too. One act of kindness can change a person's life. I never expected anything in return for my kindness, but even if I had, the return was more fulfilling than I could have ever imagined.

Years earlier, sitting in Paul Kehrer's office, I had genuinely wondered why on earth he was helping me. I now understood why: The only thing better than receiving a little kindness when you really need it is the satisfaction of knowing your kindness has the power to completely change another person's life.

BEING NICE *DOES* PAY

A 2014 paper in the *Journal of Experimental Psychology* was titled "Paying It Forward: Generalized Reciprocity and the Limits of Generosity." The authors' research supported what I had long felt to be true: When you are kind to people, they tend to pay it back. Whether that's to you directly or to someone else, your kindness reverberates out into the environment, creating a world that's built on courtesy and compassion. That's the kind of world I want to be a part of. That's the kind or world I want to create.

I gave a cup of hot chocolate and a muffin to a stranger. That interaction led me to meet a man who would, in turn, show me enormous kindness. And because of the opportunities I was able to access through him, I was, in turn, empowered to help a person who stumbled into my life at the time she needed it most. Most often, life's pivotal moments are not about luck or personal effort but simple acts of kindness. When we are kind, we take part in a vast web of connections that pulls people together and creates something bigger than all of them.

Because my own life has been so touched by the kindness of others, I've always valued relationships. Despite seeing this magic everywhere in my life, I'm constantly told the world doesn't run on kindness, and it's ridiculous to think so. You've already heard the story: "It's a dog-eat-dog world out there, and you have to be tough to survive. Do or be done. Nice guys finish last." You've heard that a million times before, right?

In my experience, this could not be further from the truth.

Let me tell you about the late Mickey Carson, someone I consider one of my earliest mentors. Mickey was a highly educated African American in his fifties, with a background in law and a way of being with people you had to see to believe. I remember being on a work trip with him once in San Francisco and noticing that wherever he went, people seemed to roll out the red carpet for him. Hotels, restaurants, conference rooms—whenever he appeared, people just lit up.

When I asked him about this, he said, "Paula, lemme give you a little advice. This will open more doors in your career than you can imagine: Every time you look at someone, look them in the eye." I wasn't impressed. That's it? "That's not all," he said. "You need to imagine that everyone is wearing a little sign on their forehead that says *make me feel important*. And then do whatever you need to do to make them feel that way."

After years of using his advice myself, I can now confirm that Mickey was completely correct. It went against the tired old dog-eat-dog trope, but treating people this way *did* open many doors for me. Today, my work as a life and career coach has proven to me again and again that kindness pays. People matter. Relationships matter. Compassion matters.

I think it's time these dog-eat-dog stories were rewritten, and I'm not the only one. For one thing, being nice does not mean being naive. Being kind doesn't mean you lack skill, intelligence, or experience, or that you're a doormat. It certainly doesn't mean you can't lead others. In fact, compassion and true empathy could be the secret ingredients for cultivating the kind of innovative leadership the world needs most right now.

Nobody illustrates this better than BlackRock Managing Director Elizabeth Koehler, winner of Bonhill Group's 2021's Woman of the Year Award (*Investment News*, 2021). At every company I've worked at, people always told me I was *nice*. Elizabeth has also been given this label, and she wears it with pride. She proves that being a strong, visionary leader and knowing how to use empathy are not opposites, but they are part of the same core skill.

The financial services industry is sadly still rife with outdated assumptions about strength and kindness and about the roles of men and women at work. Yet women like Koehler are using their platforms to show that female leadership is powerful, driven, and effective, not despite its kindness, but *because* of it.

Koehler has said in interviews that women can struggle against the way that kindness is perceived: either they're too nice, or not nice enough! In her nineteen-year career in asset management, she says her biggest challenge is navigating the

"Liz is nice" label and balancing that with the fact that she can still get results. "Don't mistake my kindness for weakness," she insists. "Because the good news is that women can be truly transformational leaders."

The key is to have confidence in your abilities and courage to express who you really are. Empathy is not something that will hold you back. Like Elizabeth, I believe it's one of the most important leadership qualities missing from today's workplaces. Maybe, right now, you're like I was on the day I tried my luck by giving the receptionist hot chocolate and a muffin. In other words, maybe you think kindness is risky, but it may be that it's riskier *not* to be kind. We all have so much more to lose by not being kind than we have to gain by being callous or indifferent.

The *Power of Nice* author Linda Kaplan Thaler believes that although kind people may be *perceived* as weak and soft, they do get things done. She points to research from Rutgers University that shows for every 2 percent increase in measured cheerfulness in an organization, a 1 percent increase in profits results. The benefits of being nice are not just financial. In her book, she explores how kind people live longer, have better relationships, and are even less likely to be sued!

Dennis Kravetz, author of *The Human Resources Revolution*, surveyed 150 companies and also found a relationship between a progressive human resource strategy (i.e., kindness) and phenomenal growth. In *The Turnaround Manager's Handbook*, Richard Sloma discovered the same thing: "People will not warm to your words if you don't appeal to their hearts."

This applies to employees and customers alike. A workplace atmosphere of kindness is a predictor of greater efficiency, productivity, and a culture of collaboration. These researchers were discovering hard evidence for what Mickey Carson had told me all those years ago: Doors open when we make people feel important.

So, do nice guys really finish last? Well, it depends on your perspective.

In my experience, there are countless ways to justify coldness and selfishness if you want to. Many people will stubbornly insist that being compassionate is a fool's game, and that they look out for themselves first because they *have to*. From my point of view, I like to remember that we always have a choice. I could have bought myself a hot chocolate and muffin that day, gone home and angrily declared that the world was a harsh and hostile place. Instead, I am grateful I chose to create kindness instead.

Had you asked me right then—as I was about to get into my car—if nice guys finish last, I might have said, "Yup! I've made a fool of myself, and I just wasted a few bucks I didn't have to spare!" Even though it took a few months, that investment of kindness *did* make a return for me, and the payoff was about much more than money.

KINDNESS IS A CHOICE

So how do you become a kinder person? Do you need to volunteer or donate a bunch of money to an animal shelter?

Maybe, but in my opinion, kindness is most effective when it's sincere and spontaneous. One of the best ways I know to be genuinely kinder is to become more attuned to what the people around you need. Then, respond to that need with a full heart and no expectation that you will be rewarded—or even thanked.

People who are naturally kindhearted are masters at noticing others and stepping in when help is needed. For example, you notice that someone is flustered and overwhelmed at work, so you temporarily lighten their load or cut them some slack. You see someone short a dollar at the checkout and reach into your pocket, or you notice your partner is grumpy so you pick up their favorite takeout on the way home from work. It's not the size of the gesture that counts, it's the fact that you recognized their need and showed you care by going out of your way to help.

Make a habit of regularly tuning into the people around you:
- Who is struggling and why? What do they need?
- Who is working hard and would appreciate your encouragement or support?
- Is there someone who could use the skills or wisdom you currently possess?
- Has anyone done something for *you* that you need to acknowledge more fully?
- Has someone shown you a lack of kindness that you could nevertheless choose to forgive?
- Is there anyone who is deliberately asking for your help? Look closely, some people have an interesting way of signaling their need for help!

If you consistently make the choice to tune into others' needs and respond kindly to them, you'll find that not only do your connections with others grow warmer, but those ripples do start bouncing back to you, and you may discover people wanting to go out of their way for you. On the path to creating the life you want, you may be surprised just how frequently kindness plays a pivotal role.

THE BIG IDEA

The decision is yours: One choice is to put your head down and pursue only your own narrow self-interest.

The other choice is to believe in something nobler than this— have faith in the power of compassion and take personal responsibility for creating a world built on trust, respect, and kindness.

It's *not* a dog-eat-dog world out there. Kindness does pay, and the research shows that compassionate people tend to live longer and feel happier. I experienced firsthand that showing kindness to others resulted in new opportunities at work and, as a result, boosted my income.

Remember my mentor Mickey Carlson's advice: smile, make eye contact, and make whoever you're talking to feel important.

If being nice is a big part of your personality, honor that at work. It will not prevent you from being recognized, valued, or rewarded, but it will be quite the opposite.

We can find success not in spite of kindness but because of it. Kindness can be a gateway to success. The smallest acts of goodwill to others can create ripples in your network that help not only those individuals but people you may never meet. The fabric of a better world is made of these small, seemingly insignificant acts of kindness.

Right now, today, what small act of kindness can you choose to put out into the world? Kindness isn't something magical reserved for the saintly among us; it's accessible to you too, this very moment. Just follow Mahatma Gandhi's advice: *"The simplest acts of kindness are by far more powerful than a thousand heads bowing in prayer."*

CHAPTER 7

BE HEALED

———

"But pain's like water. It finds a way to push through any seal. There's no way to stop it. Sometimes you have to let yourself sink inside of it before you can learn how to swim to the surface."

—KATIE KACVINSKY

CRISIS IS AN INVITATION

It was 2001, and I was twenty-seven years old. I was in America, just like I had dreamed of as a kid, and I was doing more with my life than my family back home or I believed was possible.

And I was miserable.

Although I had made it to America, I still had a long way to go in creating the life I wanted for myself. I'd lay awake in bed at night, my heart so heavy I could barely breathe. My hair was falling out, I was losing weight, and after years of running on empty, I was diagnosed with depression and told I was close to a nervous breakdown.

On one hand, when you grow up without the support and love you need, you learn to do without it. You become strong. You become resourceful. On the other hand, this way of living is not sustainable. At some point, you have to face your past, especially all the unfinished parts.

I had ignored my needs for so long that my head and heart were disconnected. I was just going through the motions, but finally, my body sent me the undeniable message: *no more.*

One of the most difficult lessons I had to learn was that you can achieve professional and personal success by all the conventional standards, but if you're not healed from your past, you will never feel whole, fulfilled, or at peace. You don't need to have had a tragic childhood; even people who grew up in perfectly "normal" circumstances may have things from their childhoods that continue to impact them. You can't build the life of your dreams if unprocessed, unacknowledged childhood pain is still haunting you. With a little courage, however, that pain can be transformed into growth.

I'd been in survival mode for so long that I simply never stopped and took stock of what was going on with me. I'd been trying so desperately to escape pain that I didn't realize what a gift crisis can be—if you embrace it.

Despite it being a completely alien concept to me, I committed to seeing a therapist once a week after a concerned friend insisted I get help. During my lunch hour, I walked over to the Medical Arts Building in downtown Minneapolis and sat down in a small room across from a woman who certainly didn't look like she cared about what I had to say. At that point in my life, I had achieved a lot to be proud of. I knew how to work hard, I knew how to learn, and I knew how to take what little I had and work with it.

It dawned on me then that I had no idea how to talk about my pain.

Run away from it? Sure, but not talk about it. I didn't even like thinking about it. In time, I would learn that my therapist really *did* care. I learned that my pain mattered.

Session after session, the therapist asked me to share memories I'd never breathed a word about—things I hadn't even fully admitted to myself. She listened. If I paused, she'd say, "Tell me more." *More*? I was baring my soul! But it turns out there was more. Once the floodgates opened, I discovered deep pools of pain inside me that had never seen the light of day.

It wasn't long before I started to crave our visits. Feeling safe and feeling vulnerable were both entirely new sensations for me. The more I talked, the clearer I could see all the wounds that had not healed yet. Wounds I hadn't even admitted were there. Some wounds were new, some old, and there were some very deep, tender ones that had been there for as long as I could remember.

I'm not someone who is scared of hard work, but I hadn't realized just how hard I'd been working to carry this enormous burden and how desperately tired I was. One session, I started crying and I couldn't stop. I cried and cried and cried for what felt like an eternity.

"Let it all out. I'm here to listen. You've been through a lot. I want you to know, you don't have to keep hauling all this weight around anymore," the therapist said. I blew my nose and stared at her. "Paula, it's like you've been lugging this heavy suitcase around with you, and some days it's so heavy you can't lift it at all. I'm here to tell you that you can put that suitcase down now. You don't need to carry it anymore."

I had only told her a fraction of my story. I could have had a million more sessions and still only have scratched the surface of my pain. In my imperfect English, how could I ever truly convey to her the depths of what I felt inside? With one look at her caring, open face I was flooded with the painful realization of just how much it meant to me that she was listening anyway. A tiny crack opened in my perception and a thin ray of light shone through. Because she acknowledged my pain, I was able to acknowledge it in myself. Let me tell you, it was overwhelming to finally face it all.

Once I did, I understood how sincerely I wanted to be healed and to be whole. I had spent all my childhood trying to escape, but in running away had I somehow left behind that young girl who felt rejected, unloved, and broken?

If you talk about childhood "wounds," well, I certainly had a long list! My mother chose not to be a big part of my life, and I never met my father. I was raised by a grandmother who treated me like I was an inconvenience. I was sexually abused by several people in my neighborhood before the age of twelve. By fifteen, I had run away from home only to marry a man nearly twice my age just six months later. I had carried all of this to America with me, keeping it all a secret. I felt I had to.

Properly acknowledging this pain was a luxury I simply did not have at the time. I couldn't afford to feel too sorry for myself, collapse into hopelessness, or dwell too long on the harsh realities of my situation. Admitting that pain would have immobilized me. So, I didn't. This is why I completely understand when my coaching clients are reluctant to go digging around in their childhoods. People think it's either a waste of time, or they're genuinely hesitant to reopen old wounds for fear of the fallout, not to mention that for many people, therapy is an expensive luxury they sadly can't afford.

Although some people dismiss therapy and the idea of "dwelling" on their childhoods, I believe that ruminating over the past is something we do precisely *because* we haven't healed it. When we fully acknowledge our pain and commit to healing ourselves, only then can we move on. What happened in those earliest years of life lives on inside us, right now in the present. Our thought patterns, our self-identity, the way we behave in relationships, all of it was first imprinted on us in our childhood years.

That pain doesn't go anywhere. We just get good at hiding it. Those wounds may then show up as self-destructive behaviors, like addictions, overeating, and overworking. Can you relate?

Despite the grand dreams I had, my ambitious plans, and my seemingly bottomless drive to reach professional success, the truth is that I never really felt *whole*. Because although I had moved on in time, and I had found ways to cope and survive—even thrive—those old wounds were still there, still hurting. I was like a knight who had covered his countless bleeding injuries with a steel suit of armor and carried on fighting.

HEALING IS A JOURNEY THAT NEVER ENDS

So, did I get therapy, sort out my life, heal all my childhood trauma, and live happily ever after?

Well, not exactly.

After working with my therapist, something wonderful happened. I started to feel better. I was so focused on healing that my improvement was drastic. In many ways, I felt better than I had in a long time. Over the course of the next few years, I continued to make progress in my career. I met an amazing man and married him, I had my two beautiful children, and my life felt like it was finally taking shape. So, I quit therapy.

Quitting therapy was a *big mistake.*

I learned the hard way that if you neglect your *continuous* healing and growth, your unresolved issues will keep coming back, sometimes with a vengeance. By 2015, I was vice president of investments at BlackRock, and my colleagues would have said I was thriving.

Yet behind that façade, I was once again facing all the same old demons. I was depressed, lost, and insecure. I also battled postpartum depression with both of my pregnancies. I could hide it from others, but eventually I had to admit to myself that I needed help again, or I should say, I *still* needed help.

It took me a long time to learn the value of professional help but a longer time to learn the value of *ongoing* professional help.

When you experience a little positive progress, it's tempting to forge ahead with confidence that you've overcome the problem once and for all. However, progress can be deceptive. You wouldn't throw out your vitamins the very instant you noticed they were helping you; in fact, feeling better is proof that you should keep taking them! In the same way, be patient with therapy, and don't quit at the moment you are genuinely starting to heal.

GEMMA NATURKACH AND THE ART OF FORGIVENESS

So, what do we do with all this pain once we acknowledge it?

Gemma Naturkach was a coaching client I first met at American Corporate Partners, an organization that provides services to veterans. At the time, Gemma was working at Microsoft in Ukraine. Many tragic things happened to Gemma growing up. However, as I sat down to talk to her about her childhood, I realized the most tragic thing was, as a child, she *didn't even realize* how miserable she was. "When you're growing up in that environment, you don't know anything else. That was just my life."

Gemma was born to a teenage mother and grew up on food stamps, along with another five children. It was a childhood rife with poverty and physical, emotional, and sexual abuse. Her mother used drugs and never worked, but she knew how to manipulate people, especially men. Gemma recalls how her mother would fall into a relationship with someone new, and she and the kids would have a little money and a place to live for a while. Eventually, she'd inform Gemma that it was time to split; they never lived in any one place for more than a year.

At the age of fifteen, Gemma came home to find her then stepfather passed out on the floor with drugs everywhere, while her mother, who was eight months pregnant with her sister, was in the bathroom high on crack and throwing up. Gemma called the police expecting help but found they cared more about where the drugs had come from than helping her or her mother. She lost her faith in the system that day, resigned to the fact that no one was coming to help.

By the young age of eighteen, Gemma had experienced extensive trauma via rape, loss of a child through adoption, and identity theft by her own mother. She joined the military hoping to make a better life for herself, but her trauma did not resolve; it only deepened. She was diagnosed with cervical cancer and while healing from surgery was sexually assaulted once again. Her commanding officer admonished *her*, telling her it wouldn't have happened "if she was a better soldier."

During this difficult part of Gemma's life, she was put on suicide watch and committed to a psychiatric ward. She recovered, but she was discharged on disability, slowly piecing her life back together at an office administration job afterward. Soon, she started experiencing intense headaches that were found to be a symptom of a pseudotumor cerebri—a swelling in the brain. Gemma can rattle off a laundry list of other disorders and a heaping dose of PTSD, as well as more adversity than anyone should experience in one lifetime.

All her life, she'd been victimized and told it was her fault. And she believed it. When something completely senseless and unjust happens, most of us make up a story to help us understand. Sometimes, the only story that makes sense is that we're bad people. But, when she realized she wasn't to blame for her past, did she blame those who *were* responsible?

Gemma's response here is unexpected. "Look, nobody ever wakes up in the morning and decides they want to be a bad person that day. Nobody makes the decision to hurt somebody. I'm sure it wasn't my old commanding officer's intention to make me have hatred for him for ten years—because that's how long I hated him for! He didn't know anything about it. But *I* felt that hate every day for ten years. He didn't."

Gemma sincerely believes that despite what it seems, everyone is doing their best. This perspective is not a favor to others, but a state of mind that allows her to release negativity and heal herself. It would have been easy for Gemma to succumb to bitterness and condemn others for the raw deal she'd been given, but she refuses to do that. Instead, she consciously chooses to focus on her values and the beautiful, meaningful, and purposeful life she wants to create.

Forgiveness is not something you do for the sake of others; you do it for yourself. Today, Gemma still battles the scars her past has left on her body, heart, and mind, but she refuses to carry any more. By going back to her past, she was able to give herself all the love, validation, and support she desperately missed out on as a child.

The irony is that going back is sometimes the only way to move forward.

HEALING THE INNER SELF

"Healing journeys do not necessarily need to be long, drawn-out processes that require years of hard work. Healing and transformation always begin with learning and discovery — the magic that feeds the dynamic, powerful inner child within."

—CARY G. WELDY

Recently, I read the late visionary Thich Nhat Hanh's book, *Reconciliation*. In this book, he claims that inside each of us is a child who is in pain. This child only does what they do because they want to protect us from further pain. When we ignore this child, that pain only deepens.

Carl Jung was the first to flesh out this concept of the Inner Child, which carries all the memories of our early experience, good and bad, from a time when we were too young to fully understand it. Children are not like adults. Utterly dependent, they look to their caregivers to provide them love, food, and stability. When the people who are supposed to keep them safe hurt them instead, it creates a wound that ripples into adulthood. Their growing selves adapt and take shape around that experience, for better or worse. That adaptation becomes their personality, their attitude, and their mindset (Fox, 1932).

When you first come into the world, you don't know the "rules." You don't yet know who you are, or what's possible for you, or how the world works, but your caregivers soon teach you. In time, you learn and you learn according to your earliest experiences with those caregivers.

I am by no means a licensed mental health professional, and I don't have all the answers, but my personal experience has proven to me just how impactful childhood can be. When children feel safe growing up, they learn their boundaries matter, the world is generally a good place, and they can expect to have their needs met. They learn they are worthy, good people. Trauma, on the other hand, teaches us the opposite. It instills unhealthy beliefs and attitudes that shape our adult experience.

What messages did *you* receive growing up?
- My opinion is not important
- I mustn't have fun, play, or show too much excitement or strong emotions
- There isn't enough
- I am never safe
- I am not worth loving
- I mustn't talk about what goes on at home
- I'm bad
- I'm not allowed to say what I want or have what I need
- I only deserve love if I'm perfect
- I should be ashamed of who I am

Here's a big question: How did your younger self adapt to cope with these messages?

If our needs routinely go unmet by our caregivers, we grow up unable to meet those needs for ourselves. Like Gemma, when others fail to protect us, we can find our own boundaries constantly re-violated in adulthood. The childhood trauma is long gone, but the *beliefs* that that neglect instilled linger on for years. This may explain why a 2017 review in the journal *Trauma, Violence and Abuse* (Walker et. al.) found that almost half of child sexual abuse survivors are revictimized as adults, which is five times more likely than average. The past is still there, repeating itself.

Big or small, a childhood wound can be pushed out of awareness, but it may pop back up in the form of low self-esteem, addictions, a short temper, self-harm, or eating disorders. Because our earliest relationships with our caregivers were the models we used to pattern all other relationships, we may find ourselves stuck in essentially the same relationship, repeatedly playing out the same drama. If we were never listened to or validated as children, we may find that as adults we don't know how to listen to ourselves. That's because we learned to dismiss our own emotional needs long ago to survive.

In her 2019 blog post, Melanie Tonia Evans—therapist and childhood trauma expert—wrote:

> *If we have received trauma that has impacted us, it not only affects our brain and our entire nervous system, but also creates embedded belief systems that form our inner identity. These traumatic beliefs become our reality and we can easily remain a victim to them because they become self-fulfilling prophecies that keep*

us replaying the same traumatic patterns and disap-
pointments repeatedly, despite how hard we may try
to avoid them.

So, where do we go from here?

First, I want to acknowledge that many people feel guilty for having lives that are relatively "normal" compared to some of the stories I've shared here. They carry shame for *not* having childhoods as obviously traumatic as mine or Gemma's. The reality is that even if you grew up with what most people would consider a happy childhood, you may still have scars and those scars still matter. You don't need to have had an utterly tragic background to benefit from the growth that comes with acknowledging your wounds.

If you suspect your inner self needs some healing, look closely at your world and the "rules" it runs on. Maybe you're a people-pleaser with deep feelings of shame and low self-worth. Maybe you're a rebel who pushes people away, or a hoarder who always feels like disaster is imminent. Maybe you're a super high-achieving perfectionist who nevertheless hates their body. Maybe you're riddled with doubt and self-criticism, forever afraid people will abandon you once they get to know you.

I know all of this sounds heavy, but here's the good news: you are **resilient**. You have the innate ability to learn, evolve, and heal, and nobody can take that away from you but yourself. Your inner self *wants* to heal, and to do so, it first needs awareness and love. Luckily, you're not alone and can seek the help of a licensed therapist.

You've probably heard of PTSD (post-traumatic stress disorder), but "post traumatic growth" is the interesting work psychologists are now focusing on. This is an exciting and more positive way to look at pain.

CRISIS IS AN OPPORTUNITY

The pain I experienced as a child left scars. Let me be clear: I didn't deserve that pain, and I didn't choose it. Neither did any of the people I've mentioned in this chapter.

But today, as an adult, I can confidently say my experiences also offered me something unspeakably precious: the chance to emerge from adversity with more compassion, more awareness, more strength, and more appreciation for the possibilities of life. Everything that happened to me made me who I am today.

I didn't grow in spite of my wounds; I grew *because* of them.

I've been surprised to find there is now some research to support this conclusion. The *Journal of Personality and Social Psychology* published a massive longitudinal study in 2019 by Seery and colleagues, which showed that the emotionally healthiest people had, in fact, experienced past misfortune in the form of divorce, bereavement, abuse, or illness. Not only that, but "people with some prior lifetime adversities were the least affected by recent adverse events. These results suggest that, in moderation, whatever does not kill us may indeed make us stronger."

Dr. Ann Marie Roepke is a clinical psychologist and consultant in Seattle. In a 2020 *Health* article, she claims, "These events can shake us and strip away our assumptions. They push you to re-examine what is most important." In other words, you learn more about yourself and life through adversity than you ever would if things had been easy. This is not to undermine the suffering; rather, it's to have the perspective that suffering and growth can go together. Suffering can be a gateway to growth.

Working with a therapist on "inner child work" is essential to help you address unmet needs and old, unhealed wounds that are echoing into your adulthood. I've personally witnessed the monumental shifts that are possible when people release old trauma. It's like removing a blockage in a river and watching it flow again.

I get it; not everyone is super comfortable with the term "inner child." I had a hard time relating to it! We can easily substitute this phrase with "healing the past" or "becoming whole." I know it can be uncomfortable to acknowledge feelings of vulnerability. I know the temptation to say, "Oh, it wasn't that bad" and shrug off the pain we felt as children. Sure, the Adult You thinks nothing of a certain event, but what did the more fragile Younger You think?

I think one of the most common ways to protect against pain is to deny any fear and vulnerability in the first place. If you frequently tell yourself, "Grow up, it's not a big deal!" realize that you may be replaying that same old pattern and rejecting that innocent child inside you who only wants to be held and comforted. What I'm saying is that sometimes playing tough might have helped us survive in the past, but it can hold us back in the present.

Dr. Tal Ben-Shahar has taught two of the largest classes in Harvard University's history, and he is the founder of the Happiness Studies Academy, where I was one of his students. He believes that to rewrite adversity into a growth opportunity, we need to embrace pain, rather than try to avoid or reject it. Writing for *Psychology Today* ("Let's Suffer from Post-Traumatic Growth"), he cites my own story when speaking about the power of post-traumatic growth.

Give yourself permission to be human, to be vulnerable, and to have needs. Take control of your own narrative. We cannot control what life throws our way, but we are always in charge of the story we tell about it. Still, that doesn't mean we have to do it alone; ask for help from a close friend or a mental health professional.

We have all we need to heal the wounds of the past: awareness, love, and the will to grow and be better every day. One of the tools we can use is an affirmation, directed at that perfectly made, younger version of yourself:
- I am lovable.
- My feelings are valid.
- I can heal and be whole.
- I am worthy of love and forgiveness.
- I am safe.

A crisis is a chance to look at newly emerging possibilities, to learn, and to reconnect to what matters.

When we are young, trauma and adversity can teach us unhealthy ways to cope. However, as adults, we can claim our right to interpret adversity in new ways. *We can teach ourselves better lessons.*

This is not to say adversity doesn't still hurt—it does! I would never suggest that suffering is good, and that everyone who hurts will find their way to growth because of it. All I'm saying is that it's *possible*. And not only is it possible to heal, but to heal and be even better than we were before.

HAVE A CONVERSATION WITH YOUR INNER SELF

We don't resolve our pain when we abstractly *talk about* it. The only way to get over that pain is to go *through* it.

Big difference, right? In other words, we are not trying to judge, understand, or justify the past; we are trying to heal it. I believe if we can do this, then trauma is transformed into something special: a doorway to growth.

How? Simple: have a conversation with your inner self. Ask your innocent, younger self what they feel and what they need. Then make a promise that you will meet that need for them.

"Long ago, I left you alone. I'm so sorry. I am going to take care of you now." Think about it: if a sad, hurt child stumbled across your path today, would you yell, "It's not that bad" and refuse to pick them up or soothe them? Would you tell them they were worthless and turn your back on them? Of course not! But when we ignore our pain, we do just that. Then we distract ourselves with social media, TV, workaholic tendencies, and other addictions, all while the inner child sits sadly in a corner, unacknowledged.

Instead, become curious about what your inner self is telling you. Ask:

- As a child, what did you always feel you were lacking?
- What did you do to survive not having that need met?
- What did you need to be told growing up but weren't?
- What "rules" and beliefs did you absorb as a child? How are they still with you today?
- If you could be your inner child's ideal parent, what would you give yourself right now?

For example, if you wished that someone had told you, "The divorce is not your fault. You did nothing wrong," tell *yourself* that, right now. If what you needed was to be heard and listened to, instead of dismissed, mocked, or shamed, listen now.

Today, I know that if you want to truly be free of the past, you need to go back and heal what is wounded and acknowledge what has been forgotten. Again, seek the guidance of an experienced professional. They can show you how to go back and collect all those parts of yourself that you lost along the way. You may discover trauma and pain go even further back than your own lifetime, and there are scared, abandoned children going back for generations. With compassion and awareness, you embrace them all, and you don't pass that pain onto future generations.

Pain, when unaddressed, becomes a block that keeps us confined in limiting beliefs in the past. We may become fragmented, losing parts of ourselves or denying our truth. When we treat ourselves with empathy and compassion, we can find those fragments, reclaim them as parts of ourselves, embrace them, and become whole again.

THE BIG IDEA

The decision is yours: In a way, it's a decision we are called to keep on making throughout our lives. The past is always with us, but we can choose how it appears. Do we want it to keep haunting us as unhealed trauma, pain, and limiting thought patterns and beliefs? Or do we want to consciously face that past, accept it, heal it, and move into the future *whole*?

Inside many of us is a child in pain. Unless we acknowledge and heal this pain, our personal and professional successes, finances, and relationships will always feel hollow—like something is missing. As painful as it can be, crisis is an invitation to look more deeply at what has been ignored. You might not want to "dwell," but you must realize that unresolved trauma (whether from childhood or adulthood) is not in the past at all, it is carried right here with us in the present.

Forgiving and letting go of the past is not something we do for others, but for the sake of our own wholeness. To heal, we ask what we had to do to survive early trauma and commit to gently rewriting that story as adults. When we are able to rework adversity into insight and trauma into evolution, we are said to be experiencing post-traumatic growth. With kindness and curiosity, we *can* heal.

How would you live today if your inner self knew they were completely loved, completely valued, and completely safe?

CHAPTER 8

GET OUT OF YOUR HEAD

———

"Life is simple. Everything happens for you, not to you."

—BYRON KATIE

"You're unintelligent and uneducated. You've been lucky so far, but that luck could run out any minute, so watch yourself. You don't belong here. They're going to find out how little you really know and then what? You'll lose everything! Who do you think you are, anyway?" For my entire career on Wall Street, nobody could have guessed these were the thoughts I was plagued with every moment of every day.

When I first encountered the work of Stanford University lecturer Dr. Shirzad Chamine and started studying how the human brain works, a light bulb went on for me: My thought patterns were at the root of everything.

At the time I was still battling the same insecurities I battled all throughout my corporate career. I was still doubtful about how I'd ever build a successful coaching business when I had never worked for myself before. I already knew I wanted to be a coach, but I had yet to connect all the dots. Enter the framework called "positive intelligence"—it was like the missing puzzle piece.

I was introduced to a wealth of knowledge and applied practices that completely changed my life. I was so convinced of the power of getting to grips with thought patterns that I enrolled in a certification program so I could offer this same insight to my clients. Becoming a positive intelligence coach has not only given me the awareness of how I've sabotaged my own well-being and happiness in the past, but also the tools to better manage my negative thought patterns. As part of my process as a coach, I now help my clients do the same.

Author and leadership expert Robin Sharma once said, "the mind is a wonderful servant, and a terrible master." When I say you need to "get out of your head," I don't mean to just stop thinking. Rather, I'm talking about stepping back from your thoughts and looking at them objectively. Your mind is a storytelling machine, and the quality of those stories doesn't just impact your life; it *creates* your life.

WHAT STORIES ARE YOU TELLING YOURSELF?

"My life has been filled with terrible misfortune; most of which never happened."

—MICHEL DE MONTAIGNE

"Once upon a time, there was a little girl whose mother abandoned her, and this made her very sad. She was raised by her grandmother, but her grandmother did not treat her well.

She was poor and alone and nobody loved her. One day she ran away and escaped forever. But her problems seemed to follow her..."

I constantly told this story to myself and others, in one form or another. It was a story in which I was the persecuted victim, and because of everything that had been done to me, I would always be that victim. It was who I *was*. Even when my circumstances dramatically changed and I built the life I always wanted, I still lugged around the same old story: I was a victim, and that's just who I'd be forever.

My early childhood experiences had imprinted a specific pattern in my psyche, which affected everything: how I felt about others, myself, the world, and especially my place in that world. I believed this story, and I dutifully acted out my role in it every day, until I realized it was just that: a story.

And a story can change.

In 2020, a team of psychologists at Queen's University in Canada (Tseng & Poppenk, *Nature Communications*) discovered the average human being has more than six thousand thoughts a day, or one thought every ten seconds. In 2005, Leahy and colleagues at Cornell University found that 85 percent of what we worry about never happens, and even the worries that do materialize tend to be managed better than expected. If we combine these findings, we could estimate that every minute you are awake, you tell yourself an average of *five* stories that are negative or repetitive in nature!

We "narrativize" so often and so easily that we seldom even notice we're doing it. We see a split-second expression on a stranger's face and have a thought. *She thinks I'm stupid.* We see an amazing coat in a shop window and make an automatic assumption. *That will never look good on me.* Every second of every day, we fill in the gaps of our knowledge according to our preexisting narrative. Remember, the research finds that this narrative is, to put it bluntly, mostly wrong!

We spend most of our brain's processing power and almost all of our time playing the same "stuck record" over and over again, and most of it never amounts to anything more than debilitating anxiety—ouch.

Importantly, this is not the behavior of some doomed pessimist; this is the normal, average human mind. It's you and me and the people we know. Humans move seamlessly through their experiences by linking events to other events, finding cause and effect, and identifying explanatory patterns. The brain is an astonishing piece of machinery and has evolved over thousands of years to do just this. Without it, we couldn't survive our world.

Survival is what it's all about. Our tendency to indulge in the "narrative fallacy" is a mental shortcut to help us make sense of the world and find order and coherence in a universe that can feel unpredictable. While experience shifts and changes around us, our story remains stable, so much so that over time it becomes our identity.

We tend to remember and emphasize those events that fit our narrative and forget or downplay those that don't. In his book *The Black Swan effect*, Nicholas Taleb explains that even though our mental shortcuts are useful, they're also usually flawed, and we perceive "past events as more predictable, more expected, and less random than they actually were." Our stories tend to collapse contradictions and flatten out nuance, allowing us to construct things in simple, binary terms. These stories are comfortable, easy, and make a kind of sense. They're also usually inaccurate.

When I truly grasped this concept, it blew my mind. My story about myself and about my past was a narrative fiction. It was a center of gravity around which all my experiences were organized, orbiting like planets. It shaped my view of what was possible, what I wanted, and what my life *meant*. Looking at my story with open eyes was like peering at the back end of life and seeing the code with which it was programmed. Things could never be the same again.

The stories we tell ourselves are *everything*.

They shape our perception, identity, thoughts, actions, and our very existence. If the stories we're telling ourselves are mostly negative and repetitive, what can we conclude? What was originally meant to serve our survival has become a trap. We are like spiders that weave a web of stories, and then get tangled in the web ourselves.

The human brain is not only built for negativity, but also to actively seek out evidence for what it already believes. If someone looks at me on the street, I am not perceiving their expression neutrally. Rather, I'm interpreting it in the context of my story. If my story is one of judgment and anxiety, I will see unkindness in the stranger's face.

Thus, my world makes sense. I tell myself that people don't like me, and everywhere I look I magically find evidence. When the next person I encounter on the street smiles at me, instead, I dismiss it. It doesn't fit the narrative. What *does* fit is that they were probably laughing at me. So that's the story I tell. The story "people don't like me" becomes the longest running blockbuster film in my world, played on a loop, and I don't even know it. It is, as far as I'm concerned, the truth.

When we bring awareness to our stories, we get the chance to direct a different film. We can cast ourselves in different roles and rewrite endings. Do you want to know how to change every single thing in your world? *Change your story.*

So according to Leahy et. al., more than 80 percent of the thoughts running through your mind today are the same old thoughts you had yesterday.

What would happen if you thought something different?

WHY YOU HAVE IMPOSTER SYNDROME

When we encounter something that doesn't match our narrative, we experience a temporary loss of coherence. I know of no clearer picture of this disparity than the now well-understood phenomenon of imposter syndrome. Why do seemingly successful people feel like they're actually horrible failures? Because the story they're being told by the world doesn't match the story they tell themselves (maybe six times a minute).

On the one hand, they have outward markers of success: awards, promotions, recognition.

On the other hand, they have their old narrative that says: "you're unintelligent, you don't belong, and you don't deserve anything."

How on earth do you make the two fit together? Here's the "explanation": you're secretly a fraud, and your success was just a lucky fluke. The emotional momentum of the narrative is maintained. Even though your life is objectively successful, you still say, "Nope. I'm unworthy." If I'm undeserving of success and I'm successful, it must be through some means other than my deserving it, right?

We could spend time trying to live *inside* the narrow confines of these stories, or we could step *outside* them and ask what kind of life they're creating for us.

I was fascinated to read the original 1978 research on imposter syndrome by Clance and Imes—yes, it's not a new idea! They were interested in certain high-achieving women who seemed to doubt their own accomplishments and felt completely unable to reconcile their success as something that belonged to them.

Today, there are countless books, conferences, and talks aimed at helping women get to grips with feeling like a fraud. Famous and accomplished women like Michelle Obama, actress Charlize Theron, and Sheryl Sandberg have admitted to experiencing it. Even the esteemed Supreme Court Justice Sonia Sotomayor said once in a 2019 NPR interview, "I am always looking over my shoulder, wondering if I measure up." Though the term was originally focused on women, I'd like to stress that men experience imposter syndrome too. They may just feel ashamed to say so.

The mismatch between reality and the stories we tell about reality goes much further than imposter syndrome. How are *your* personal narratives playing out in your life? How accurately do these stories align with reality?

POSITIVE INTELLIGENCE: REWRITE THE STORY

"Your mind is your best friend, but it is also your worst enemy."
—SHIRZAD CHAMINE

Recall that the "normal" human brain churns out six inaccurate stories per minute. Frankly, this state of affairs is not in our best interest. Exactly how we can commit our minds toward our highest potential instead is the focus of the positive intelligence theory, or PQ.

Just as physical fitness improves our well-being, so too does mental fitness. If we're not mentally fit, we lack cognitive and emotional resilience, and, simply stated, life is more difficult.

The mastermind behind the theory of positive intelligence is Shirzad Chamine. In his seminal 2012 book *Positive Intelligence: Why Only 20% of Teams and Individuals Achieve Their True Potential and How You Can Achieve Yours,* Chamine explained that human beings have essentially two minds working at once:

1. The more ancient primordial brain that evolved to focus on survival. This is the root of all self-sabotaging behaviors and the habitual thought patterns he called "Saboteurs." *This part of your brain usually sabotages you.*
2. The positively intelligent brain which approaches challenges with creativity, curiosity, joy, empathy, gratitude, and problem-solving. It's the home of the "Sage." *This part of your brain works in your best interest.*

In Chamine's theory, the so-called Saboteurs are your entrenched thought patterns, that is, the stories you tell, which shape your world. For example, if you believe "I'm unintelligent," you may experience shame and imposter syndrome when you succeed. The Sage is the part of your brain that argues against this sabotage. Through conscious awareness—being awake to what is happening in your mind and why—the Sage challenges stale old stories and fosters positive feelings, helping you solve problems in healthy, adaptive ways.

Your early childhood experiences instill habitual patterns of thought within you. You maintain your identity by constantly repeating these patterns, and this repetition shapes every inch of your life. When Chamine analyzed more than two hundred scientific studies, he found that those with a higher PQ experienced better marriages, better health, better professional performance, and better overall success in multiple areas of life.

Our mental fitness is determined by the relative proportions of these two: Is the Sage or the Saboteur getting the most airtime? Or to ask it another way, is your mind your master or your servant?

Whatever your answer to that question, rest assured that with every new moment, we are all given a brand-new chance to set down our old patterns and choose something different. Every time we resist our Saboteurs and choose empowering, positive thoughts instead, the scale tilts a tiny bit toward the life we want.

MEET YOUR SABOTEURS

I have tried many, many times in life to "be better." I've wanted with all my heart to let go of my suffering and genuinely change, once and for all. I'll be honest: Most of these attempts failed, and that's because I didn't properly understand why that suffering was there in the first place. I didn't understand how my brain worked, and so it continued to work against me.

I believe that the hunger for transformation is inside everyone, but as long as we're working *within* our habitual patterns, instead of changing those patterns themselves, we'll never find any lasting change. Insight is not enough. Good intentions are not enough, either. We need to consistently train our mental fitness, design our life with purpose, and deliberately cultivate the thought patterns that will help create that life for us.

We don't have to let the same tired old stories run the show. My own self-talk was often about being worth less than others, and this shame seeped into every relationship, every action, every word, and every emotion.

What are your Saboteurs?

Chamine identified nine overarching patterns in how we orient toward life. Think of them as story genres:

1. **The Judge**, which is the master Saboteur and finds faults with self, others, and circumstances
2. **The Stickler** manages anxiety with perfectionism and extreme attention to detail
3. **The Victim** may be unconsciously attached to problems, playing martyr or exaggerating suffering as an unconscious bid to win affection
4. **The Avoider** flees from difficult and unpleasant tasks and conflicts by procrastinating
5. **The Hyper-rational** finds solace in logic, but can be felt by others to be intellectually arrogant and cold
6. **The Restless** is busily planning for the next exciting distraction, one foot always out the door
7. **The Controller** believes, "Everything is up to me, and I can't mess up"
8. **The Hypervigilant** is constantly focused on danger and what could go wrong
9. **The Pleaser** thinks they only have worth if they serve others' needs
10. **The Hyper Achiever** thinks, "That last achievement doesn't count; I still need to do more." (Chamine, 2012).

We all have our own unique constellation of Saboteurs, and our stories can take on one main theme or blend a few together. Whenever I did well at work, my Saboteurs were there waiting for me. The Stickler, The Hyper Achiever and The Pleaser all jumped in: *You don't know what you're doing. You call THAT an achievement? They're going to find out you're a fraud any day now...* Any time you find yourself living in this kind of "quiet desperation," trust me, you're buying into your Saboteurs' lies. Could you listen to your Sage instead?

Every one of us is born with a gift and the possibility of achieving their fullest potential here on this earth. We can all make a difference. We can all contribute. I want to tell you, this doesn't happen unless we decisively remove what is standing in the way, undermining our well-being and robbing us of our potential. Our Saboteurs feed us a story about how the world works and who we are. They say, "you need to be like *this* to survive." But they're lying. As long as we believe those lies, we will not reach our full potential.

My Saboteurs told me I was worthless and didn't belong anywhere. They said if I wanted to be happy, I needed to make as much money as possible, be worthy of others' love and friendship, and prove I *could* make something of myself. Even after I had ample evidence that I was a strong and accomplished woman, I still felt bad about myself. It was because I had been lied to. According to Chamine,

> *90 percent of the valuation in people's happiness from one person to another is explainable based on what is happening inside of their own head, not based on what's happening in their life in terms of wealth and possessions or any of that stuff. [...] Your unhappiness has nothing to do with what's happening in your life. Your unhappiness comes from the fact that you are not in command of your own mind (Chamine, 2012).*

In other words, their positive intelligence quotient (PQ) decides their happiness, not their talent, wealth, or luck.

The more I talk to the people I most admire and respect, the more I agree with Chamine's assessment. I've seen intelligent, talented people waste their enormous potential because of self-sabotaging loops.

We all have a Sage, even if we're in the habit of not listening to it. This is the true self we were born with. Unlike the Saboteur, this voice always tells the truth, and you can always trust it. It has your best interest at heart, and it wants you to grow and learn and find joy and purpose in life in the uniquely wonderful way only you can.

How do you know which voice is which? The Sage is the voice of calm, positive authenticity. It *feels* good. The voices of the Saboteurs, however, all seem to pivot around anger, fear, and regret. This is the voice of a bully.

You came into this world brimming with potential and possibility. Have you ever asked a young child what they want to be when they grow up? You'll see the Sage's strength and beauty in their free and outlandishly ambitious answers. This is what we were all like before the Saboteurs came and dimmed the light in us. I'm not saying the Saboteurs don't have any value. In my case, they pushed me to do more than I ever thought possible. Having the tunnel vision that comes with being harassed by your Saboteurs can make you pretty effective! It won't make you *happy*, though.

To be happy, I had to take a serious look at my stories, and they were rewritten.

DEFINE YOURSELF

When I think of the people who've learned how to win the game with what looks like a bad hand, I can't help thinking of my friend Josh Rudman. Josh is a likable guy in his twenties who started out answering phones but worked his way to vice president of investments, and he continues to rise in the ranks despite his youth. I first met him working at BlackRock and he is hands down one of the hardest working people I know. He agreed to talk with me about labels, self-sabotage, and defining oneself.

You wouldn't immediately guess that Josh's grandparents were Iraqi Jews who were driven from their home country during the Holocaust, and who arrived in 1930s America without a word of English and empty pockets. Talking to Josh today, you can't quite imagine he's ever felt insecure. Yet he was born with severe dyslexia, which felt like *two* obstacles in one: the first being the practical impediment to learning, but the second being the fact that he was labeled "stupid" before he was old enough to even know what that meant.

When Josh was a kid, the realization that people thought he was somehow lacking as a person left a deep wound on his developing psyche. While Josh saw his parents idolize his conventionally intelligent brother, he was put in a class with kids who had far more severe and debilitating disabilities. He thought, *Is this what I am?*

Labels are a funny thing. They're actually stories and foregone conclusions about how our lives are supposed to play out according to the roles others assign us. Josh's label caused his teachers to drastically underestimate him, but it also meant they didn't challenge him when he was lazy or defiant. Josh was branded a problem kid, so that's what he became.

Your story might not be like Josh's, but we all receive messages from parents and teachers in our early years about our worth and what is possible for us. "This is who you are, and you'll never be better than this."

But whose story is it?

Although Josh had a "learning disability," he ultimately demonstrated the ability to learn a bigger, meta-lesson: People can define themselves. For Josh, the thing that prompted him to break free was nothing more than the desperate urge to prove wrong everyone who had underestimated him. Call it competitiveness, pride, or downright stubbornness, but Josh discovered he could take people's doubt in him and use it as fuel to be better.

People told Josh early in life, "You can't do it." Something defiant inside him said, "Oh yeah?"

Many successful people begin life this way. They feel like they need to constantly prove themselves. At first, it's an ego game and a reaction against feeling insecure. If you're stubborn, lean into that and use it as fuel to help you achieve what you want for yourself. Still, something funny happens when your doubters spur you on and you actually do succeed—you realize you no longer need their approval and, in fact, you never needed it.

It's then that you wake up and realize that you control your own narrative. Your success doesn't rest on external limitations or the beliefs and attitudes of others. Like Chamine discovered, it rests within *you*.

Josh realized he didn't have to convince anyone of his worth or win their validation. He didn't have to ask permission to hold himself to a higher standard or take other people's perspectives as gospel. We all have our demons, but you can choose whether you want them to define you. Could *you* define *them*? What happens if, like Josh, you change the story, and reframe your flaws and weaknesses as strengths and opportunities?

Step away from people who are quick to downplay your success or celebrate your weakness. Step away from those who don't believe in you before you take on their perspective as your own. If you don't have a support network around you just yet, that's not a problem. If all you have right now is critics and Saboteurs, consider yourself lucky and dig deep into the feeling of indignation and the desire to prove them wrong. Their underestimation of you may be worth more than you know!

THREE STRATEGIES FOR BUILDING POSITIVE INTELLIGENCE

"Between stimulus and response there is space. In that space is our power to choose our response."

—VIKTOR FRANKL

STRATEGY 1: WEAKEN YOUR SABOTEURS

First, understand why your Saboteur is there in the first place. What survival function does it serve? How did it help you cope with early life challenges?

When I was rejected by my mother, I could not make sense of it. How can a mother reject her child? The answers are complex. Sometimes, there are no answers and bad things happen to innocent children for no reason.

That the world is a chaotic and senseless place is a heavy thing for a kid to carry. That's why my Saboteur was born. My Saboteur told me my mother must have abandoned me for a reason, and the reason was because I was a bad child. This is an excruciating idea, but it helped me cope because it offered me a way out: If I could be good, I could win back the love.

My Saboteur helped me make sense of a senseless situation and helped me survive. When I understood this, I could say with awareness, "Thanks Saboteur, I can see you're trying to help, but go away." Your Saboteur is not your enemy! We can let go of its outdated lies when they no longer serve us, while still appreciating that they did serve us and our survival.

STRATEGY 2: STRENGTHEN THE SAGE

If your Saboteurs have been running the show for a while, the Sage perspective may seem radical. When we shift our thoughts into Sage perspective, we are able to convert every circumstance into a gift or an opportunity. We feel empowered to choose, explore, and create, and we're not shackled to what has been in the past. After all, that path is not yet decided. *It's yours to chart.* How empowering is that?

A Saboteur nags on and on about how difficult life is and how it *must* be that difficult. It decides what it wants to believe, and then it does whatever it can to make that so. The Sage is free. It doesn't jump in with assumptions and old narratives, but simply asks, "What's this? And how can I turn it into a gift or an opportunity?"

If you notice yourself getting carried away with the Saboteur's same old boring nonsense, pause and ask your Sage to weigh in. Show some self-compassion by asking yourself, "what is the kindest thing I could say or do toward myself right now?" Then become curious about the next step you can take.

STRATEGY 3: PQ REPS

The positive intelligence version of walking ten thousand steps a day for good health is to do one hundred "PQ reps" a day. One rep means bringing your attention to one of your five senses in the present moment for around ten seconds (or three breaths). Every day is bursting with opportunities to do this—like right now as you read! Simply pause and become aware of your body and the sensations you're experiencing. One easy way to do this is to rub your fingertips together so gently and with so much focus that you can feel the ridges of your fingertips.

Hyper focusing this way can both strengthen the Sage and weaken the chatter of the Saboteur. It takes practice though; just as thinking about walking doesn't improve your physical fitness, reading and thinking positive things doesn't improve your mental fitness.

You might be wondering, is there no room for negative experiences at all? Isn't it useful to be a *little* self-critical?

Chamine is quite clear on this: shame, despair, and fear *are* useful but only to a point. Around 5 percent of that suffering is necessary and has a function; the rest is just a mass of pointless loops. It's the same as touching a hot stove. You don't need to keep your hand in the flame for two hours to understand what the solution to your problem is. One of the Saboteurs biggest lies is that your life *needs* to feel bad. It doesn't (Chamine, 2012).

Here's an exercise to try as you go about your day. As often as possible, become aware of your thoughts and whether they're *driven by the Saboteur or the Sage*. Simply notice your self-talk and where it's coming from. What purpose does it serve right now? What purpose did it serve in the past? I'm not going to tell you to magically start thinking like a Sage overnight; it's enough at first just to become aware. Just open up a little space and become curious; what would it be like to tell a different story?

THE BIG IDEA

The decision is yours: It's a straightforward one: Do you want to live out the same old story, or do you want to see if a new, better story can be written? Do you want to let your Saboteurs direct the narrative of your life, or your Sage?

We have over six thousand thoughts a day, most of them repetitive and negative. These thoughts shape everything—who we are, what we feel, how we behave—so if we can change them, we can change our lives.

Our brains are wired to tell the stories that help us survive, but what worked in the past may no longer work now. We need to enlist the help of our wiser selves, the part of us that has our highest interests at heart. Shirzad Chamine's theory of positive intelligence helps us understand these two guiding narrative forces in our lives: our Saboteurs and our Sage.

To increase our mental fitness, we need to cut the airtime we give to our Saboteurs and strengthen the Sage by doing one hundred "PQ reps" a day. As you finish this chapter, what thoughts have bubbled up in your mind? Did these thoughts come from the Saboteurs or the Sage?

If you need support becoming more mentality fit consider reading *Positive Intelligence* by Dr. Shirzad Chamine or *Breaking the Habit of Being Yourself* by Dr. Joe Dispenza, or else consider seeking help from a positive intelligence coach.

CHAPTER 9

OWN YOUR TRUTH

———

"The truth will set you free."

—JESUS CHRIST

SWEET LITTLE LIES

The Bible says the truth is supposed to set you free. Well, the truth is, I had been telling lies all my life.

I don't mean to say I was always dishonest, but I wasn't exactly living in truth, either. How often did I see the truth, *my* truth, and choose to turn away from it? How often did I stuff my genuine experience into a too-small box and pretend it was something else?

For most of my life, I wished I was someone different. I wished my parents had loved me. I wished I was happy, successful, and confident. I wished I had money and felt intelligent. I grew up in a country with a massive chasm splitting the rich from the poor. The upper and middle classes never mixed with the poor unless they were being provided with a service.

Some of my earliest memories are of serving people "better off" than me. To put food on the table, my grandmother washed clothes for middle-class families, and I'd clean houses and sell rugs after school for extra cash.

I don't know exactly when I learned that being *us* was something to be ashamed of, and being *them* was something to envy, but even as a young kid, I was already telling people elaborate stories designed to conceal who I really was and make them think I was one of them. When asked at school why nobody ever saw my mom or dad, I'd cheerfully say my parents traveled a lot for business.

In my life, I've experienced four marriages, three divorces, three emigrations, countless jobs, grinding poverty, depression, and a good sprinkle of physical and sexual abuse. As you say in America, I came from the wrong side of the tracks. I didn't take the easy, beautiful path through life, and I never felt I was one of "them." That's why I always carried the belief that if anyone knew the real me, I'd no longer be good enough to be part of their lives. So, I'd lie.

Here is the big lie that spawned all the others: I was fundamentally unworthy, undeserving, and just plain bad. Everything I'd been through, all the pain and fear I'd tasted, the dangerous roads I'd traveled, the tender hopes and dreams I'd kept alive in my heart—all of this was *not enough*. If I wanted a chance to one day eat at the table with the happy, educated, respected, and well-off people, I'd have to keep my real self a secret. I genuinely thought the only way I would be good enough for them is if I was someone else.

What I know now is that this couldn't be more wrong.

The longer I kept my secrets, the stronger they got and the weaker my spirit grew. The more I denied who I was and my past, the less of me there seemed to be.

I want to share a truth I had to learn the hard way: If you forfeit who you genuinely are in exchange for a more palatable lie, you're always getting a raw deal. If you want to build a beautiful life for yourself, you have to do it as the person you genuinely and actually are. *You have to own every single part of you.*

THERE'S NO TRUTH WITHOUT VULNERABILITY
So why all the lies? To put it simply, fear.

Being honest is risky because it asks us to reveal ourselves, our *real* selves, to the world, where we might be judged and hurt. Instead, some of us have made an unconscious bargain: "I'll pretend to be who I think I should be, and in exchange I won't have to risk being rejected."

It's a bad bargain, however, because in forfeiting our vulnerability, we also abandon our truth. We abandon *ourselves.*

When we accept that *all* our experiences, good and bad, have made us who we are, we are free to be in the world as the whole, three-dimensional, beautifully complex people we are. When we are present in life as ourselves, *all* of ourselves, we live fearlessly, enjoying the brilliant clarity of knowing what we want and having a chance to be at peace with that.

We build a life on a strong foundation of truth, instead of on the quicksand of lies.

Not only does embracing vulnerability allow us to live in truth, but it allows us to connect more deeply with others because we connect with *their* real vulnerable selves and not with the pretend version they've chosen to present. When I am real with people, it gives them permission to be real with me. When I show up as my full self, I make space for the other person's full self, too. We can truly connect. It may not be glossy and perfect, but it's something better: It's *real*! It's no longer a superficial connection between mask and mask, but something deeper, more satisfying, and with the potential to heal everyone it touches.

I had it backward for so many years when I thought being flawed and vulnerable makes you somehow ineligible for connection with others; in truth, it's a necessary condition for it! Vulnerability makes connection possible. Vulnerability is the wellspring of joy, connection, and creativity—all of it. What's more, we don't need to earn the right to connect by being worthy; we are already worthy, right now.

Close to six years ago, I watched Brené Brown's famous TED Talk on shame. It was the first time I heard someone accurately describe the weight I had been carrying around. She also helped me realize that this baggage was getting in the way of something that really mattered to me: meaningful connection. According to Brené Brown, in an article titled "Shame Resilience Theory: A Grounded Theory Study on Women and Shame" published in 2006, human beings are built for connection. It defines our very being.

Yet look at people's stories of *dis*connection and you may find the thought, "Some parts of me are not worthy of connection." How can we connect if we aren't willing to be seen? There is a painful sense of vulnerability behind all this that ironically shuts us out from the thing we most desperately want.

Honestly sharing vulnerable parts of yourself is never easy. I'll let you in on my secret agenda, though; I'm hoping that *my* story, once told, can go out into the world and do some good. If any part of my story can help you with yours, then every back road I took and every bump in the journey to be where I am today was worth it. That makes any embarrassment, judgment from others, or self-doubt a small price to pay.

THE POWER OF OWNING YOUR TRUTH

"The privilege of a lifetime is to become who you truly are."

—CARL JUNG

Be honest. In your world, is "professional success" actually secret code for "be less you"?

Owning your truth is a radical shift. It means we are whole, and we act from that wholeness. We live lives that are in alignment with our deepest truths, courageously speak our heart, and have integrity. We do all of this not from some perfect place we hope to be someday, but from where we are right now, *as we are right now.*

When we heal, we call back to awareness the old parts of ourselves we lost or disowned years ago. Honesty can heal because when we speak the truth, we are whole again. We don't have to be perfect to be well; we just need to be *whole.*

Our culture seems to feel that if we're successful enough, we don't have to suffer the indignity of being vulnerable anymore, that is, if you make it to the top of the pile, your past doesn't matter anymore, right? "Just as soon as XYZ happens, then I'll be someone worthy of love and happiness, and *then* I can be authentic. Just let me push a few things under the rug first…" I can assure you, this is a lie, too.

The Latin root for the word courage is *cor*, which means "heart." The older meaning of having courage was the ability to "speak one's mind by telling all one's heart" (Brown, *Daring Greatly*, 2012). The courage to be imperfect is the courage to speak your heart, even when that truth is small, uncertain, or afraid. Though it's not our conventional definition of strength, it takes immense integrity to release the vision of who you think you should be and embrace who you *actually* are.

HOW SHAME FUELS INAUTHENTICITY

"Shame" according to Carl Jung, "is a soul eating emotion" (Mayer, 2017). It may sound dramatic, but I have since learned that your soul can also be eaten away in tiny nibbles. Every time you hide yourself, fail to speak up, or quietly wish you were someone different, that's a bite. Every time you look at your magnificent, unique, and precious life, and pronounce it "not good enough," that's another bite.

Shame is not the feeling that we've *done* wrong. Rather, it's the feeling that we *are* wrong—big difference.

But if we devalue ourselves this way, we no longer trust our own judgment and we abandon our unique gifts, perceptions, and desires; instead, we submit to other people's truths. In other words, we behave inauthentically. We quietly confirm the unconscious belief that *our* truth is not worth fighting for or even acknowledging. *At the core of much inauthenticity is shame.*

What does shame and inauthenticity look like in *your* life?
- Have there been times when you wanted to speak your truth but didn't?
- Have you substituted your own genuine perceptions, desires, and goals with someone else's?
- Are there parts of yourself you deliberately keep under wraps because you believe they aren't fit to be seen?

According to Brown's Shame Resilience Theory (SRT), shame is endemic, but the way to combat it is not with more shame. Instead, shame shrivels when exposed to light, empathy, and acceptance.
- Instead of keeping secrets, share your truth.
- Instead of silence, speak up.
- Instead of judgment, have self-compassion.

Even if some parts of us don't feel worthy of love, those parts are still there. Untold truths are still true. Shame resilience means we can hold *all* parts of ourselves with empathy and choose to authentically connect with others exactly as we are, right now.

We don't have to find vulnerability *comfortable*. We just have to acknowledge that it's necessary. In my experience, this acknowledgment brings about a deep relief that is the first step toward living authentically.

DON'T LIVE YOUR LIFE BEHIND A MASK

Whose life are you living?

So many people have been acting out a role for so long that they don't even know who they are anymore outside of that script. When I was younger, I thought my task was to adjust myself until I fit my environment as closely as possible. All my life, I had been *wrong*, but if I had the *right* job, the *right* connections, and lived in the *right* neighborhood, maybe I'd feel better.

Like Thomas Merton once said, "People may spend their whole lives climbing the ladder of success only to find, once they reach the top, that the ladder is leaning against the wrong wall." When you begin a journey by denying your truth, you might be surprised to find how unrewarding the final destination feels. To some extent, I'd succeeded in doing all the right things. Yet fulfilling society's idea of success didn't fulfill me. Why? Because it wasn't my own.

I didn't need to adjust myself. There was nothing wrong with who I was. What was missing was my acceptance of what I knew, deep down, to be my truth. Instead of changing myself to fit the environment, I needed to find the environment that aligned with who I genuinely was as a person.

What did I need? Who was I? What did I want my life to be?

Dr. Chad and Dr. Shelley Prevost are the founders of Big Self School. In their 2022 blog post titled "How to Live in Your Truth: The Difference between Personal Values and Social Conditioning," they explain the difference between social values and your own, personal values. When we're younger, we may automatically internalize the fears, goals, and beliefs of our caregivers and society.

Others tell us what it means to succeed, who is worthy, and who isn't, and this secondhand story becomes a truth we live. We take those goals as our own and start walking the walk, not quite realizing that it was never something we consciously chose for ourselves. The world says, "this is what it means to be successful," "this is what you need to be happy," and "this is how you should look to be beautiful." We listen and act accordingly.

The truth is, it can be hard to untangle yourself from this societal conditioning and ask what kind of life *you* want. Some of us wait decades before asking that question! What is *your* true self? I don't honestly know. I do know, however, that you have a set of gifts and a purpose here on this earth, and it is your job to do the inner work to find out what they are. This is work worth doing.

Researcher Kennon M. Sheldon, in an article titled "Becoming Oneself: The Central Role of Self-Concordant Goal Selection," finds that being true to yourself is a question of "self-concordant goal selection." In other words, the ability to choose a life path that aligns with your values, not somebody else's. "To be true to oneself," he says, "is to consciously refer to one's stable values, motives, and beliefs as one makes decisions, which can be difficult when momentary social influences are insensitive or contradictory to these values and beliefs" (Sheldon, 2014).

A licensed therapist can guide you in this. Choose someone you trust and like, and who can hold your journey as you do the sometimes-delicate work of learning to be more vulnerable. There's a perception out there that therapy is only for those of us who are really messed up, right? I think the opposite is true. Asking for professional support shows courage and a willingness to invest in ourselves, not because we're damaged and need to be fixed, but because we value ourselves and our growth.

I've been with the same therapist for years now—the wonderful Dayna Hopko—and the work we've done together has been invaluable. I would not have grown as I have without her support, as well as the expert guidance of the life and career coaches I have worked with.

BE BRAVE; BE HONEST

"You cannot live a brave life without disappointing some people. But those people who get disappointed, it's really okay. Because the people who care for you, who are rooting for your rise, won't be disappointed. That's how I make myself brave."

—OPRAH WINFREY

Any time we take a leap of faith into the unknown or we dig deep and evolve, we need more vulnerability, not less. This is because we're not the only ones who are squeamish about dealing with the raw, unedited, vulnerable parts of the human experience. We all belong to cultures that run on unspoken rules about what is and isn't allowed to be expressed, felt, and acknowledged.

When you speak the truth, you may encounter resistance. In stepping away from the conventions of your society and crafting the life *you* want to live, you may be surprised to find you trigger defensiveness in others.

Learning to speak my truth was and still is truly scary for me. I'm still very much a beginner. I was even hesitant to write about this topic here—out of fear of what people would think. I am facing my fear and not letting it drive me, but I also know there's a good reason people are inauthentic. There's a reason people say being authentic is "brave." It's because going against the grain is unpopular. To be frank, sometimes people would prefer you didn't shine all that light into the dark corners, thank you very much!

If people reject or belittle your efforts, or if they act as though your striving for healing is a personal affront to them, try to understand that that's about them, not you. It can sometimes feel like owning your truth actually stirs up even more shame and judgment from others. Countless times, I've found myself in conversation with someone who casually says something like, "he's not very stable, he's been married a couple of times before" or "I can't believe she's dating that guy, he's uneducated and never went to college." Hearing comments like these kept me locked in my jail of lies, never telling people the truth about my past.

If this is your experience, I want to remind you of something important: The world *needs* your authenticity—speak up. Some people might even argue that it's selfish to keep your gifts hidden! That's because *behind your truth, lies your hidden gifts.* There are people out there who share your struggle, and when you bring that struggle to light, you can't help but bring a little light to theirs, too. In shrugging off your burden of inauthenticity, you make the burden they carry a little lighter. Please don't think that claiming your own value will harm others. It's never selfish to speak your truth or to authentically be who you are.

GALEY ALIX'S STORY: NOT PERFECT, BUT WHOLE

"Perfection is a toxic desire. We are not supposed to be perfect. The challenge is not to be perfect, it's to be whole."

—JANE FONDA

Galey Alix has accomplished much in her thirty-odd years, but her trajectory did not follow the path she thought it would. Not long ago, she was engaged to be married to a tech CEO, decorating her new ten thousand square foot home, and preparing for a dream life she thought she was meant to lead. But as she battled the demons of OCD and disordered eating, her relationship crumbled and she found herself in a deep depression. For Galey, owning her truth meant bravely walking away from it all.

In an attempt to heal herself, she started decorating homes on the weekends and sharing the videos online. These makeover shorts quickly went viral, and she's now under contract with a major network for a docuseries about her life and her special brand of DIY. Today, with over five million social media followers, it's fair to say she's created a beautiful life that others admire. That's why it's hard to believe her when she told me in an interview that her life has been riddled with self-doubt and inauthenticity.

Often, I hear this story: when people have a core belief that they are not enough, they feel compelled to prove themselves and do twice as much to win the love they don't feel they deserve deep down. They may feel unable to rest until everything is controlled, optimized, and perfect (remember The Stickler?). Healing is not in finding perfection, but in realizing that they were never unworthy in the first place.

It was during this painful crisis point that Galey began to wonder, where had this kind of thinking gotten her, anyway? She felt the hunger for authenticity. She yearned to be loved for who she was—and she'd have to go first! No more would she pick herself apart or chase people who were bad for her. It was a lightbulb moment: perfectionism created misery. She was done with perfect. She wanted what was *real*.

She gave herself permission to be vulnerable and talk about her mental health, and this gave her fans the courage to do the same. It was a revelation. She had wasted so much time covering up the brokenness she felt inside, when what she craved was just being herself, out in the world, and being seen and appreciated for who she was—warts and all.

Now, whenever she can, Galey shares the message that it's beautiful to be flawed.

Working on Wall Street, running her own design business, managing her social media, selling her own décor line, and being the executive producer on her TV show, today, Galey is certainly still very busy, but now, the control freak is no longer in charge.

Galey is proof that working with our imperfection yields much more growth than denying our vulnerability.

DON'T BE PERFECT, BE YOU

I've told you a little about my own truth, but now it's your turn. Even if you can only be honest with yourself for now, try answering this question, and answer it from the depths of your truest, most authentic self:

What would it look and feel like for you to own your truth?

Then, think of small ways you can start to do this in your everyday life.

- See what it feels like to admit to others when you're afraid or unhappy. Notice their response; is it what you expected?
- Own up to your mistakes and honestly acknowledge when you don't know the answer. "I don't know" can be so liberating!
- Without apologizing or downplaying your needs, ask for help when you genuinely require it and see what happens.

- Speak out against something you know is wrong but haven't had the courage to yet. Does it make you feel more or less fearful to speak up?
- Think of a secret you've been carrying that has been acting like a cancer in your soul. Identify someone you trust to practice your truth with. Notice how you feel before and after sharing.

Imagine a world where we all had the courage to own our truth and to cheer on and support those who did the same, instead of tearing them down. Where everyone believed, "I am enough." A world filled with more radical honesty, more compassion, and more deep connection where it matters. Well, I believe that world is actually possible, and it's happening right here with us.

THE BIG IDEA

The decision is yours: You have one life, and it's happening right now. Do you want to live that life behind a mask or behind a lie? Or do you want to live that life as *yourself*? You are, after all, the only person in the world qualified to do so!

The truth will set you free, but lies and secrets will enslave you. The only real way we can create the lives we want for ourselves is to do it genuinely, as the people we are. This takes the courage to be vulnerable, but if we are brave enough, we can discover that vulnerability also opens us up to deeper, more meaningful connections with others.

We don't have to be perfect, or fearless, or have it all figured out. We just have to show up as ourselves with sincerity and the willingness to speak from the heart. It's this, and not perfection, that gives meaning and direction to our lives.

Being honest is not always easy, so expect resistance! If you are courageous, your life will be richer, more connected, and more purposeful. I promise.

"As we let our own light shine, we unconsciously give other people permission to do the same."

—NELSON MANDELA

CHAPTER 10

BE GENEROUS

―――

"So what?"

That's the nagging thought that kept popping up in my mind. It was 2018, and I was working my dream job at BlackRock, living a life even more successful than I had ever dreamed of as a child, but all I could think was, *"So what? Who cares?"*

It was dawning on me that even though I had achieved everything I set out to, and more, there was *still* something missing. For years, I had worked my butt off proving to myself and to my grandmother that I could be somebody, and now that I had done all that, what was my purpose? What was the point of it all?

The new questions I found myself asking were unexpected. Even more unexpected was where I eventually found the answers: at the company I was working for.

Larry Fink is the founder and CEO of the world's largest investment manager, BlackRock, the company that employed me. Heading a business with almost $10 trillion dollars under management, Fink is regularly named one of the world's greatest leaders, and he continues to challenge and inspire world and corporate leaders, including myself.

In a 2018 letter to shareholders and Fortune 500 CEOs, Fink claimed that if an organization wanted to thrive, it needed to identify its purpose. "Without a sense of purpose, no company, either public or private, can achieve its full potential." He explained, "Your clients need you to show leadership. We need to go far beyond profit and find ways to contribute to the wealth and success of not just shareholders, but the entire community. More than ever, successful business owners need to take on a bigger, more important responsibility. In other words, they need to give" (*Forbes*, 2018).

Fink was addressing the heavyweight CEOs and leaders of the world, but at that moment, it felt like he was speaking directly to my personal dilemma. The challenge he laid down was crystal clear. What was I doing to better the world I lived in? It hit me like a thunderbolt: nothing.

I immediately talked to my incredible leader, Tom Pfeifer. I told him I needed to go further and do something far beyond my current role. I wanted to be a part of making the world better, and I wanted purpose. He connected me with a colleague, Tim Miller, in California, and together we informally started a giving initiative. Inspired by my husband Randy's mission trips and the words of Larry Fink, Randy and I along with Tim Miller and thirteen others decided to cross the border to Mexico and help poor families build homes.

The poverty I witnessed there stunned me. Here were people living in homes consisting of little more than torn tarps and dirt floors, and I was fretting over how hollow my success felt! It was a sobering—and more than a little embarrassing—reality check. The first people we worked with were a family of seven living in Ensenada. The BlackRock team worked with them to entirely rebuild their dilapidated home from the ground up. Bear in mind, I had never even picked up a hammer before!

We built more than a house on that trip; we each left with a deep, renewed sense of purpose. I cannot adequately describe the thrill of knowing that your actions are creating genuine good in the world. That feeling was so intoxicating that on the way home I immediately committed to doing even more. In the two years that followed, I helped co-lead eight similar trips, and I am now planning to return to give back with my sons.

Larry Fink was right. Purpose is everything, and I can think of no greater purpose than to serve others. Did we help those people in Mexico? We absolutely did. The reality for me went much further, however, because the same year this mission trip initiative was launched was an especially meaningful year in my career. I won three different awards, but none of them had anything to do with my sales results at BlackRock. Instead, they were all about having an impact well beyond profit. This all came from my renewed sense of purpose and the passion I was now able to bring to that purpose.

My purpose had changed. In the past, it was all about professional and financial success. More than anything, I had wanted to make something of myself so that back in Brazil my grandmother wouldn't need to wash other people's clothes for money anymore. Yet now, on the way back from our first trip out to Mexico, a new clarity and awareness began to form in me and my mission quickly shifted.

Deep inside, I knew I needed to change careers; I wanted to become a professional coach. More than anything, I wanted to have a real impact on the world and help others achieve their potential. This exciting new sense of purpose was a direct result of what I first gave.

A beautiful magic happens when you give. I've seen it. I've felt it. It doesn't always make conventional "sense," but the act of generosity lifts and ennobles everyone who takes part, whether they're the giver or the receiver.

What's more, the people who have most inspired me on this long, hard journey have done so not because of how much value they could ultimately extract from those around them, but from how much value they added. It might sound strange coming from someone who grew up impoverished, but I know in my deepest heart that life's meaning is not measured by what you get, but by what you give.

ARE YOU A GIVER OR A TAKER?

"Sometimes when we are generous in small, barely detectable ways it can change someone else's life forever."

—MARGARET CHO

Consider this scenario: You and a stranger will both receive some money. You have three choices about what you and the stranger will receive, and you'll never see or meet the stranger. Which option would you choose?

1. You get five dollars and the stranger gets five dollars
2. You get eight dollars and the stranger gets four dollars
3. You get five dollars and the stranger gets seven dollars

In business, takers are everywhere. Takers are all about what they can get. If there are no consequences and you'll never see the other person, they reason, why wouldn't you get the most you can and choose option 2? This question comes from organizational psychologist and author Dr. Adam Grant's quiz, which is designed to see whether you're primarily a giving or taking person. Grant has been Wharton's top-rated professor for seven years, and he has published several books, including my favorite, *Give and Take: A Revolutionary Approach to Success.*

He surveyed tens of thousands of people across the world and found that most of us have a "matching" style—we choose option 1. The idea with this style is that you balance give and take; you scratch my back, I'll scratch yours. Makes sense, right? Happiness Academy founder and author of *Choosing the Life You Want: The Path to Conscious Happiness,* Tal Ben-Shahar, outlines Grant's three styles:

- **Givers.** People who give without expecting anything in return. Their motivation is to help and make things happen.
- **Matchers.** They balance their giving with what they receive in return.

- **Takers.** People primarily interested in receiving and getting as much as they can from others.

Do you think I'm about to say we should all choose option 3 and give more than we get? Well, Grant conducted a study on salespeople in North Carolina and calculated their "giver scores." This metric was simply a measure of how much the person helped others versus promoting their own interests. Grant discovered that while takers and matchers seemed to score somewhere in the middle performance-wise, the least successful salespeople were all high-scoring givers.

So, does that mean being a giver is a bad idea? Interestingly, Grant found something else: the best performing salespeople were *also* givers! They averaged 50 percent more annual revenue than all those takers and matchers in the middle (Grant, 2014).

What are we to make of this study? Does being a generous and giving person help or not?

Well, it turns out that this may not be the right question to ask. Givers tend to be on the extremes of performance and are overrepresented at *both* the top and the bottom. So, how are successful givers different from unsuccessful ones? The key may be in them finding a way to help others generously while also pursuing their own interests.

Consider the fact that Grant found that most people are matchers, so that's the kind of person you are most likely to encounter in life. If you're a selfish taker, this eventually means the consequences are going to catch up with you, since most matchers will tend to penalize that kind of behavior, even if it benefits you in the short term. You might get away with initially stealing credit for someone's ideas, for example, but soon people will match your behavior and you may find yourself mistrusted and shut out of collaborations, or even that others are more willing to disrespect your work in the same way.

If you're a giver and you encounter a taker, you may well get taken advantage of, at least in the short term. But what if you're a giver who encounters a matcher or even another giver? Well, magic can happen. Generous people may take longer to get there, but they do reach the top, and their success is lasting and real.

THE MORE YOU GIVE, THE MORE YOU HAVE

According to entrepreneur Adam Rifkin, balance is key, both on an individual and organizational level. You don't have to be a saint. Just find small ways to add value to people's lives, i.e., "five-minute favors" (Forbes, 2013). Share what you know. Connect people. Give positive feedback and do it without compromising your boundaries.

Many people are worried that being a giver will be taken for granted by others, who will take and take until there's nothing left for you to spend on the projects that matter. Nonetheless, Grant has spent his entire career nominating others for awards, writing letters of recommendation, and offering valuable feedback to those who ask. After a day of lectures, he describes regularly coming home to three hundred emails in his inbox—all asking for help, which he gladly gives.

How?

Grant is not naive. He understands that burnout is a real possibility, but for him, it's a question of mindset. "I never get much done when I frame the three hundred emails as 'answering emails.' I have to look at it as, *'How is this task going to benefit the recipient?'*" You see, Grant is not focusing on what he is losing by giving; he is focusing on the deeper value, and this fills him with satisfaction and fulfillment.

It's not just fulfillment though. Harvard Business School Professor Michael Norton and colleagues found in their 2008 study that when his participants gave money to someone else, it boosted their sense of well-being more than if they had spent that money on themselves. Funnily enough, this was counter to what the participants themselves predicted! A 2006 study by Rachel Piferi and Kathleen Lawler discovered that people who helped and supported those around them had lower blood pressure than those who didn't.

When you give, you foster meaningful connections to others and reduce stress levels. What's more, generosity is contagious, and when you give, your kindness ripples out into your network and beyond. University of California's James Fowler published a study in 2010 in the *Proceedings of the National Academy of Science*, showing that when one person was giving, others were inspired to do the same to different people. Even if you never know it, your kind act today could spawn hundreds of people you've never met to do a good deed.

University of Arizona's Nathan Podsakoff conducted a meta-analysis of thirty-eight studies across a range of industries and discovered a pretty reliable correlation between employee giving (or "citizenship behaviors") and overall business success—better efficiency, customer satisfaction, lower turnover, and increased profits.

In 2006, Jorge Moll and colleagues at the *National Institutes of Health* found that giving to charities creates a warm fuzzy feeling you can literally measure in the brain. The parts of our neuroanatomy associated with pleasure, trust, and feelings of social connectedness are all flooded with endorphins, creating something like a "helper's high" that understandably boosts physical health.

No wonder that on their blog *Gatesnotes* Bill and Melinda Gates described their *Giving Pledge* project to donate billions of dollars of their wealth as *fun*. "Even before we got married, we talked about how we would eventually spend a lot of time on philanthropy," Gates wrote in the foundation's annual letter. "We think that's a basic responsibility of anyone with a lot of money. Once you've taken care of yourself and your children, the best use of extra wealth is to give it back to society."

True, Bill and Melinda have now divorced, but notice that their vision of philanthropy nevertheless survives. Notice also how there isn't any self-sacrificing martyrdom in their statement. Gates speaks plainly about using his resources to take care of his priorities first. So, it is never a question of your needs *versus* other people's needs. They both matter! There's an important mindset shift from *either/or* to *both/and*.

Being a selfish taker doesn't work for you or anyone else. Then again, neither does recklessly over-giving and burning yourself out. We can achieve our goals and be ambitious, *and* we can help other people do the same. We can collaborate and support and serve others, all without it taking away from our own development. In fact, like Bill Gates, the more we succeed, the more we have to offer others.

CAN YOU GIVE TOO MUCH?

"If you want happiness for an hour — take a nap.
If you want happiness for a day — go fishing.
If you want happiness for a year — inherit a fortune.
If you want happiness for a lifetime — help someone else."

—CHINESE PROVERB

Adam Grant is proof that being generous does not sentence you to a life of being a doormat or underachiever. In his 2014 book *Give and Take: Why Helping Others Drives Our Success,* he describes the opposite: At thirty-one, he is the highest rated and youngest-tenured professor at his university, and in his seven-year career, he has published more high-caliber research papers than many peers have in a lifetime. He has advised the world's biggest and most innovative companies, and he is a *New York Times* bestselling author with seven books that have been translated into thirty-five languages.

He is also a fanatically giving and generous person, and he will tirelessly go out of his way to do things for others that have no direct benefit to him. His life, in other words, turns the "nice guys finish last" story on its head. That's because Grant understands that generosity is *not* the opposite of productivity; it may, in fact, be its engine and a vast and untapped wellspring of good feelings, motivation, purpose, meaning, and energy.

We shouldn't ask, "How does he manage to give so much and still have enough left over?" This is framing things from a taker's perspective! Instead, he is productive *because* he is giving. He knows that giving doesn't take away from who he is, but adds to it. Takers end up creating the very dog-eat-dog world they think they live in, whereas generous givers find, paradoxically, that the more they give, the more they seem to have.

We need to change how we define success. It's not about competition, about winning or losing, or about zero-sum games. It's about contribution. It's about the bigger picture and the meaning and value we bring to life.

Can we give too much? This question only makes sense when we frame giving as something that diminishes us. If we see giving as an honor, an opportunity, and a way to find personal meaning and richness in life, then no, we can never give enough.

The people I know who are at the top of their game are not takers, but they are not martyrs either. They have a special relationship with generosity. For them, generosity is not transactional or merely done with some expectation of reward later. Rather, the giving *is* the reward. It's not in what they do, but the spirit in which they do it.

FOUR WAYS TO GET AHEAD BY GIVING

I want to share four ways you can start finding this mindset shift in yourself.

1. TEST YOURSELF

Are you a giver or are you a taker? You can take Grant's quiz, "Give and Take" for yourself on his website at www.adamgrant.net. A great first step is to build self-awareness and become conscious about how your attitudes and actions affect others.

2. BE KIND… FOR FIVE MINUTES AT A TIME

Use Adam Rifkin's "5-minute favor" technique and find something generous you can do right now that costs you nothing:

- Introduce two people in your network
- Reach out to people you've lost touch with and show an interest in their lives
- Deliberately ask someone how you can be helpful
- Donate to a good cause or volunteer time, resources, or expertise
- Challenge yourself to random acts of kindness: leave money in the parking machine, give a stranger a genuine compliment, do a favor for your spouse, or put in a good word for the new hire
- Share what you know or offer valuable advice to someone who needs it

3. VOLUNTEER IN A WAY THAT MEANS SOMETHING TO YOU

Remember that it's not about doing what you expect to be rewarded for or doing what looks good to others. Rather, it's about finding your own satisfaction and meaning in building a collaborative, abundant world.

So volunteer for a project that genuinely speaks to you. The next time you find yourself complaining about a frustrating problem or issue in your world, stop and take action instead.

Who needs help? What do you have that could be of service? What solution do you want to be a part of?

I dedicate 20 percent of my coaching hours to organizations and individuals I believe in, like American Corporate Partners (ACP), which serves Veterans and their spouses, and Grad Life Choices because I love the work they do for young people and I want to be a part of the changes they're making possible.

4. CLUMP YOUR KINDNESS

In one study, Adam Grant asked one group of study participants to "clump" together five acts of kindness every week for six weeks and another group to disperse their kind acts randomly throughout the week. Those who grouped their kindness acts together experienced a bigger endorphin rush, which means two things: they felt better, and they were more likely to want to keep being kind, which benefits others. If you can, find a way to pack all of your good deeds together!

Finally, although I think that generosity that blooms from the best parts of us can never be wrong, we do have to practice discernment and take care. It is in nobody's interest to be completely selfless. Your self-interest and well-being are a part of the puzzle, too! Volunteer and give generously, but don't be afraid to ask for help yourself or to be strategic in how, when, and what you can devote.

"You have not lived today until you have done something for someone who can never repay you."

—JOHN BUNYAN

The decision is yours: Will you be a taker, a matcher, or a giver? Will you choose to see life as an exercise in getting as much as you can, or are you willing to shift perspective and see what new possibilities generosity can open for you?

Life's meaning is not a measure of how much you get, but how much you give. Giving generously is good for others, good for us, and good for the world we wish to create.

You can get by fine in life by being a "matcher," but if you consciously choose to be a giver, magic can happen. Make the mindset shift and see that giving doesn't take away from your happiness, but adds to it. By going from "either/or" thinking to "both/and" thinking, we find ways to meet our own needs **and** give generously without burning out or becoming doormats.

Rather than seeing generosity and compassion as a threat to productivity, see it as the *source* of productivity, and the real secret to getting ahead. Rather than something that undermines your finances and well-being, generosity is a wellspring that strengthens both. Giving allows you to create meaning and purpose; what do you have to contribute, and how can you start sharing that with others around you, in your community, and beyond?

CHAPTER 11

BE GRATEFUL

―――

"As we express our gratitude, we must never forget that the highest appreciation is not to utter words, but to live by them."

—JOHN F. KENNEDY

Nobody owes you anything.

But there is an unexpectedly beautiful flip side to this; knowing I was entitled to nothing taught me to cherish what I did have. The ironic thing about growing up with very little is that you really understand that you could have had much, much less. I had my fair share of adversity, but on the other hand, I could have ended up on the streets, homeless, and addicted to drugs. This fate was never something abstract for me; all around me, I saw people who weren't so lucky.

Growing up with very little gives you an unexpected edge, which is that you seldom feel entitled to anything. This means you're primed for gratitude. I'm grateful for *everything*, both the peaks and the valleys that have made me who I am today. I will continue to live my life expressing gratitude to God, to the kindness of good people, to the country I chose to make my home, and to the country I was born in.

In the previous chapter, I spoke about generosity and giving, but for me, the desire to give back and the appreciation for everything I have been given are really the two sides of a valuable coin. Having my own life so transformed by people's generosity planted a yearning in me to make a difference in the lives of others.

I'm still learning so much, but what I'm certain of is that the quality of your life is determined by both your generosity and your gratitude, by both your thankfulness and your service. Two sides of the same coin.

THE OTHER SIDE OF THE COIN

In what ways is your life, as it is right now, positively bursting with blessings?

I want to assure you: You are blessed—enormously blessed. Gratitude is just the awareness of this fact!

Remember my trip to Mexico? I came home from that trip buzzing. Even though nothing had changed in my material circumstances, I felt more fortunate than ever. It was an interesting surprise that when I gave a lot, it made me realize just how much I had to give. Giving made me more grateful. Being grateful made me want to give even more. Today, I understand that a big part of creating the life you want for yourself is realizing just how blessed you are with the life you already have. It's also about helping others to create the life they want for themselves.

Professor Robert Emmons and Michael McCullough founded the *Research Project on Gratitude and Thankfulness* and they discovered that gratitude is not just a nice idea, but has a myriad of measurable benefits, like better health, more optimism, and improved self-esteem.

Emmons is the world's leading gratitude expert, and he has popularized the concept of the gratitude journal, which he claims has benefits for not only mental and physical health, but also for our sense of connection with others. He told *Greater Good Magazine* that although some people can dismiss the practice as too basic, "in our studies, we often have people keep gratitude journals for just three weeks.

Yet the results have been overwhelming. We've studied more than one thousand people, from ages eight to eighty, and found that people who practice gratitude consistently report a host of benefits." Those benefits include:

- Stronger immune systems
- Lower blood pressure
- Less pain
- Better sleep
- Improved mood
- Greater alertness
- Lower feelings of isolation
- Feeling more helpful and generous

"Gratitude is a social emotion," says Emmons. What I love is the beautiful and reciprocal dance between gratitude and generosity: The more thankful we are, the better we feel and the more we give, which makes us feel even better.

What do I mean by gratitude, anyway? When we turn attention to what we are thankful for, we're not saying that our difficulties and burdens don't exist. All we're doing is acknowledging what we *do* have and choosing to focus on what is good in our lives and in the world.

I think it goes even further. When we see that a source of goodness can come from outside of us, we are suddenly hit with a pleasant humbling; we realize we are dependent on others, and our well-being is not just down to our own selfish striving. In place of scarcity and competitiveness, the world suddenly seems brimming with gifts. You develop the opposite of paranoia, pronoia, where you believe that the world might be secretly conspiring in your favor!

A 2009 study in the journal *Personality and Individual Differences* by psychologist Alex Wood and colleagues, suggested that gratitude had an enormous impact on overall well-being: an impact more powerful than individual personality differences.

A study published in the *International Journal of Workplace Health Management* titled "Virtues, Work Satisfactions and Psychological Well-Being among Nurses" also showed correlations between gratitude and a range of positive outcomes, including less fatigue, more proactive behaviors, better job satisfaction, and fewer days lost to absenteeism.

Dwelling in gratitude seems to neutralize feelings of envy, shame, and resentment, and it purifies your intentions. With gratitude, you are more resilient, recover from setbacks, and emerge from adversity looking for the upside.

Your perspective comes with an automatically higher sense of self-worth, without needing to lower the worth of others.

How would you feel if you knew that not only were your gifts needed and appreciated in the world, but that others were willing to contribute their gifts to you, too? How would you act? The research shows that, like giving, being grateful changes your brain, releasing feel-good neurotransmitters that positively influence your mood, literally training your neural circuitry to focus on what's going well.

That's not all. What's good for people's brains is also good for businesses that want to employ those people.

Can you guess the number one reason people leave their jobs? The answer is that they probably feel undervalued. A Gallup poll found that employees who don't feel recognized are twice as likely to resign in the following year than those who do. If you can show your employees gratitude and give them the chance to demonstrate gratitude to one another, you give them purpose. You boost motivation and satisfaction, and while it'll help the bottom line, the benefits go much further than that (Mann & Dvorak, 2016).

MINDING THE GAP, FINDING THE GAIN

"Comparison is the thief of all joy."

—ELEANOR ROOSEVELT

Back in 1988, legendary entrepreneurial coach Dan Sullivan launched The Strategic Coach Inc., and first identified what he called "the gap" (Sullivan, 2022). He noticed that when high-achieving people dismiss their achievements, they usually do so because of a belief about what they should have achieved. Their unhappiness comes from the gap between where they are, and the yardstick they're measuring their performance against.

You devalue where you are because you're constantly measuring against where you wish you were, that is, you have a big gap. You might also experience "hedonistic numbing" so that no matter how good things get, you always move the goalposts, immediately taking what you have for granted the second you acquire it.

We all have reference points against which we measure ourselves. A lot of the time, though, those reference points are external, and we didn't choose them consciously. By now, we all know social media is a comparison tool, and marketing is designed to put us in a perpetual gap and keep us there. Operating in relation to these destructive reference points means we never measure up, and so we always feel bad about ourselves.

When you are in the gap, you tune out your inner voice and disconnect from your values. Yet at some point, you have to stop chasing and ask if the goal is what you really want. This is precisely what many of the people interviewed in this book did. Do you want to keep devaluing your past and discounting your genuine experience? Do you want to continue to neglect to acknowledge and celebrate your accomplishments right now because they don't live up to some moving target you have in your head?

When you live in the gap, you're dissatisfied by default. When you live according to someone else's reference points for meaning, you're automatically ungrateful. According to Dr. Benjamin Hardy, co-author of the 2021 book *The Gap and The Gain* with Dan Sullivan, you need to completely remove external reference points and do something else: live in "the gain."

When you're in the gain, you don't measure against someone else's yardstick. Instead, you reference against *yourself* and where you were before. That's the real metric for you, and the only one that doesn't devalue your experience.

Josh Waitzkin wrote in his 2008 book *The Art of Learning* "what did I believe three months ago that I no longer believe today?" With this perspective, you start to not only see progress, but appreciate it. That progress means something because it is about you and you alone. What's more, when you reference against yourself, your heart is open to gratitude. You can look back on your journey and appreciate how far you've come.

So many of us zoom in on the one thing we *didn't* do today. This is a form of ingratitude. Why devalue your day this way and dismiss the dozens of things you *did* achieve? For me, gratitude is about so much more than appreciating the sunset now and then. It's about shifting your mindset so that you stop running yourself ragged chasing a horizon you can never reach. Instead, you focus on what you have, who you are, and how exactly you're going to squeeze every last drop from this gift you've been given called life.

JASNA BURZA: A LESSON IN BEING THE LIGHT

"Learn to light a candle in the darkest moments of someone's life. Be the light that helps others see; it is what gives life its deepest significance."

—ROY T. BENNETT

Jasna Burza is the kind of person I feel like I knew once a hundred years ago, in another lifetime. A refugee who made a life for herself in America as an entrepreneur and now business coach, Jasna has lived a story that's all about resilience, overcoming, and the connectedness of everyone on this earth.

Like Kimberly, Gemma, Kevin, and myself, Jasna had to grow up quickly. Looking back, she still can't quite believe how any human being could survive what she went through. When I sat down with Jasna to talk about this long journey, she spoke plainly and with conviction, telling me she came to this earth for a reason and that reason continues to evolve.

When she was eight years old, war broke out in her hometown of Livno, Bosnia. When the bombing first started, Jasna was visiting with her uncle and cousins. They fled immediately. For three months, they stayed in a Croatian refugee camp, eventually reuniting with Jasna's mother, brother, and sister. In the meantime, men over the age of eighteen, including Jasna's father, were sent to concentration camps while the women and children fled to escape the threat of being killed or raped.

She remembered her time in the camp as a frightening, hungry one. Her mother, brother, and sister had no idea whether

her father was dead or alive, and she felt like nobody in the world cared in the slightest what happened to her. Occasionally, she'd get a glimpse of the world outside on a TV and how it carried on oblivious to her suffering. She felt like they were considered "garbage people" and their lives didn't matter. *She* didn't matter.

When they eventually returned from the refugee camp, her father was nowhere to be found. Jasna describes a village of bewildered women with all the men missing. There were rumors that they were being held in forced labor camps, moving rocks in a river in the middle of winter. For five long years, it was a constant struggle to get enough food, flee bombs and grenades, hide in shelters, and do whatever it took to survive.

There were no plans, no future, just survival.

Her father finally did return home, but he'd been tortured and came back a changed man. He had gone in young and strong, but he came out old, gray, and violent. He had always been an angry person, but it was around this time, when Jasna was nine or ten, that the domestic violence started. For her father, the war was still going on. After all, he was alone with his undiagnosed and untreated PTSD and forced to live in the same village as the people who had tortured him.

For years, the country was in shambles. The economy was destroyed, houses were dilapidated, and humanitarian aid was barely holding things together. Faced with ongoing chaos and pain, it was a daily challenge to find any sense of normalcy. The family had lost their jobs, possessions, everything.

But Jasna's mother was a woman of faith, and taught her that no matter what, you take care of people. Even in the midst of despair, her mother kept a small flame of goodness and hope burning.

Today, Jasna exudes a sense of gratitude and humility that people who encounter her find hard to reconcile with the horrors she experienced. She believes that, although she can't explain it, she has been guided. Through the times when there was no light, no hope, nothing of value at all, there was still something that couldn't be snuffed out. Jasna doesn't know how to describe it. "I just saw a possibility," she says. Despite everything, there was good in people. There was good, period.

She had always been the book smart kid who helped others with their homework, and so the idea slowly blossomed in her mind: *What else can I do?* She was around fourteen when she discovered something that many adults never discover: When she did good for others, she felt amazing.

This vision of a better life energized her and gave her purpose and power. At fifteen, she started a youth organization that brought together three warring communities—Protestants, Muslims, and Catholics—on the belief that she knew something better was possible.

She learned to use a computer and eventually secured funding to travel. Though her English skills amounted to what she learned watching the American TV show *Melrose Place,* at fifteen, she got a job as an interpreter for the Organization for Security and Cooperation Europe (OSCE). She'd attend school in the morning, then skip her afternoon classes to go to work. For three years, she was the sole breadwinner for the family.

Over time, her English improved, and she slowly earned more money. She had her eye on a youth scholarship to help people come to the United States to study conflict resolution, and by the grace of God, she got in, along with thirty-six others.

One day, during the course, she was asked a question.

"What are you going to do with your life?"

The man asking the question was philanthropist Dan Whalen, who Jasna regards as a remarkable human being. "Dan Whalen gave me my life." That day, he saw something in Jasna and offered her a full four-year scholarship to one of the best colleges in the country.

That act of generosity completely and permanently altered the trajectory of Jasna's life.

When Jasna speaks about her good fortune, her perspective gives me goosebumps. "I know that my life could have been so much different, Paula. There are so many incredibly talented, beautiful women in Bosnia, who never got the chance that I did. And it's a chance I worked my butt off for! I studied hard, and I was a straight A student. I did all the right things. But it was because someone gave me a chance."

What her benefactor taught her was that once your needs are met, it's your responsibility to ask, what now? What do

I want my life to be? Beyond the money, what is my legacy? What's the point?

For someone whose childhood was marked with abuse and hunger, Jasna is proud to say that today she has everything she has ever wanted. She's grateful for the good times and for the hardships, and she's grateful that she is successful enough to have the privilege of paying her good fortune forward.

She takes this responsibility very seriously. There may have been a time when she felt like a "garbage person," but someone looked at her and saw the goodness in her, saw that spark of potential, and wanted to protect and nurture it. Is there anything more valuable in the world than that? Could you ever put a dollar value on something so profoundly generous?

Generosity can change the world, but so can gratitude.

In the end, we are all connected, and we all come from the same place. I'm blown away by Jasna's faith in humanity, and I hope I've done my part in sharing with you the gift she has given me.

GRATITUDE IS A HABIT
"Counting your blessings" is old advice, but it's good advice. Here are some easy ways to start cultivating more gratitude today.

Write a gratitude letter
Taking the time to put in words exactly how great it feels to be helped by someone is a perfect way to strengthen those

gratitude feelings. You don't have to send it, but if you do, be prepared for the warm fuzzies to multiply!

Do a gratitude visit
When was the last time you intentionally honored someone who contributed to who you are and where you are today? It's easy to think of someone in your family or immediate circle, but what about others who have made a significant difference in your life's path?

I've had many special people who arrived at times when I needed them most. In May of 2021, I made a kind of pilgrimage to visit my first employer, Paul Kehrer, and his wife, Esther, in Laramie, Wyoming. I got to look each of them in the eye and tell them just how much I appreciated everything they'd done for me. It's a moment I'll never forget.

Daily gratitude practice
Every night, I write down three to five things I'm grateful for. Even recognition of the tiniest gifts can cause a seismic shift in your attitude. I felt myself feeling more optimistic and more proactive. All I was doing was noticing how incredibly blessed I already was. I wasn't any more blessed than I had been before, it's just that I was no longer cheating myself out of appreciating all those things! For the past two years, I've used a "5 Minute Journal" from *Intelligent Change*, and it's not an exaggeration to say it's changed my life.

If you notice an ungrateful thought or dissatisfaction pop up or you find yourself complaining, gently turn your attention to something that is working. Get out of the gap and look at how far you've already come. Can you think of a few achievements that you're proud of right now?

Don't get too complacent and list the same thing over and over. Keep it fresh and try to find new things every day. Keep alert and expect that the world has a little present waiting for you, if you just keep your eyes—and your heart!—open.

Create a gratitude ritual
If journaling isn't your thing, try a more concrete ritual every day to remind you to open your heart to thankfulness. You could have a "gratitude jar" that you fill up with loose change. Every time you add a coin, focus on how fortunate you are. Pause and think of your blessings. When the jar is full, donate it to someone in need. You'll find that old pocket change gives you a return you were not expecting.

Another tip is to prolong the positive experiences you have every day but might be taking for granted. Stop and really savor your food. Say a little prayer when you wake up, thanking God for how amazingly comfortable your bed is. Practice the Stoic technique of "negative visualization" and imagine your faithful coffee machine wasn't there every morning to provide you with a delicious cup; then notice how much more you appreciate that cup, instead of drinking it on autopilot.

THE BIG IDEA

The decision is yours: It's a question of where you put your attention: one choice is to focus on the negative and everything that's missing from your life. The other is to realize instead how truly blessed you are right now and to continually choose to embrace this abundance with a thankful heart.

Giving and gratitude are two sides of the same coin. When we practice gratitude, everything in life improves, including our careers. We can cultivate more gratitude by staying in the "gain"—appreciating how far we've already come—instead of dwelling in the "gap"—constantly comparing ourselves to where we think we should be.

When we live our lives with both gratitude for what we have and the willingness to share it with others, wonderful things happen. Today, simply take time to notice the positive impact of certain people and things around you and imagine they weren't there. What would it look like to express gratitude to these things?

"Acknowledging the good that you already have in your life is the foundation for all abundance."

—ECKHART TOLLE

CONCLUSION

——

THE PATH FORWARD

We all make decisions, and writing this book doesn't redeem me from mine.

It was not okay for me to marry a man almost twice my age. It was not okay for me to divorce not just once but three times. It was not okay for me to be dishonest about my past, or to work myself into a breakdown, or to endure relationships that weren't good for me. Back then, I was completely lost and looking for help in all the wrong places, hoping a savior would come along and fill the hole in my soul. I do have compassion for that version of myself, but I want to be clear that while I accept and own my decisions today, I don't claim that what I did was *right*.

I was raised by a fire-and-brimstone conservative Baptist, so believe me when I say I know what it means to feel guilty and ashamed about the mistakes you've made. My decisions may not have been good ones, but they were *mine*. When I could accept that, I understood that no matter what has happened in the past, we all have the power to choose something different today.

I would never, ever want my own kids to choose what I did. At the same time, these choices taught me lessons that created the person I am today. They taught me that no one has the power or responsibility to make you happy; that's your job. My choices taught me that secrets and lies are cancer to the soul. They taught me that just because change is scary, it doesn't mean you can't do it. Finally, they taught me that there is a heavy price to pay for not owning your truth. A price that is simply too high.

Can you achieve success without a formal education? Assuming the career you chose doesn't require specialist training like medicine and law, for example, then yes, absolutely! While I achieved great levels of success without a formal education, I do believe my life could have been much easier with one. It's much harder to keep insecurities in check without something external to validate your abilities. Still, even though the road may be rockier, it can still be traveled, and it can still take you where you want to go. As always, the route you take is yours to choose. Choose wisely and own the consequences because one way or another, every choice is a potentially pivotal moment.

In this book, I've told you many stories—my own and others'—about those pivotal moments that define a life. Those times when we ask the question that unlocks everything, and we are suddenly on a cliff edge, ready to leap off and fly. In these moments of adversity, confusion, and pain, we realize what is *really* standing between us and the life we want: the single decision to make it so.

I believe we are always just one decision away from creating the life we want.

To end, I want to tell you one final story. It was early 2019 and I was sitting across the desk of a powerful and yet humble man. It was Rob Kapito, co-founder of BlackRock, one of the most powerful companies in the world. It goes without saying that I was nervous!

He had agreed to meet with me and my colleague, Tim Miller, and we were planning to ask him to support our efforts leading mission trips to Mexico to build homes for the poor. The likelihood that anyone at any company would land a meeting with someone that important is pretty much zilch, but there we were, in a beautiful top floor office at BlackRock headquarters in New York City.

I looked at Mr. Kapito and asked him, "What was a defining moment in your life that made you the man you are today?" He looked at me puzzled, probably wondering what that question had to do with the Mexico project. There was a long silence, and I could see he had gone off somewhere in his memories before finally looking at me and answering,

> *When I was thirteen, my father had a stroke. I didn't even know what a stroke was. We grew up in upstate New York, and we didn't have much money and life was hard. My mom brought me to the hospital to see my dad and he couldn't use one side of his body*

anymore. My family didn't have any money to get any help, so the only option my mom had was to send my dad to a veteran's home—and they are not the best healthcare facilities in the world. It was our only option, but by 2 a.m. that morning, we were able to get him in.

When I visited him, he was in a ward with forty other people, some with legs and arms missing. Dad couldn't talk. He couldn't walk. And we had to leave him there. I remember turning around when I left and seeing a sign on his bed: Bed #5. That was the best we could do for him.

That was a defining moment in my life. That night, I made the decision that I had to do better for my family. That's why I went on to do what I did. Hospital Bed #5 was the moment I made the decision to go after what I wanted for myself and my family. And I did.

Rob Kapito tells a story not dissimilar from the stories you've already heard from Galey, Jasna, Kevin, Gemma, and others. In fact, it's not all that different from my own! Like them, from a very young age, I knew that if I wanted my life to change, I was going to have to make it happen. I was going to have to take responsibility, be brave, and work hard for my dreams, no matter how difficult the path proved to be. It was my decision to make.

Once I understood that, I was free to create my life the way I saw fit. Since I was a child, I'd felt cursed by my lot in life, riddled with shame and doubtful of what was possible for me. But whenever I ask the truly inspiring people that walk among us about trauma and adversity, they all tell me the same thing: it doesn't matter. What matters is what is born from that adversity. What matters is your courageous ability to be here now, in this beautiful moment, and to fully embrace your total responsibility to move forward.

The path forward has not been forged yet. *You* choose the next step.

Why did I choose to focus on these specific principles?

I'll admit, I'm a self-improvement junkie, and I've read countless books on what it takes to achieve success. However, I never found any that focused on what it takes to be successful *and* feel whole and fulfilled at the same time. I learned the hard way that true fulfillment doesn't exist without healing from our wounds of the past. It can't happen.

In my own journey, I learned that although you can achieve outward success, it does not necessarily translate to feeling whole or healed. For me, feeling that I was enough and always have been enough was not something separate from my career and financial success; it was the foundation of that success!

This book focuses on the key principles to success and fulfillment, but from a place of authenticity, healing, and vulnerability. Too many of us resist working on this because we don't want to dwell; we want to keep forging ahead! It's sometimes easier to *not* feel, right?

You can do that if you want to. I did that for most of my life. But I always felt like there was a hole in my soul, like something was missing. It's a lie we tell ourselves. We tell ourselves that we will work on ourselves and heal the past but not until we achieve success. The truth is, today I look back and wonder how much *more* success and happiness I could have experienced if I had not waited so long.

I didn't know any better, but after reading this book, I hope you will.

Each brave person highlighted in this book embodies a principle that was key to their success and fulfillment. However, it's not just about what they did, it's also about what they didn't do.

Whether in the stories of my interviewees or of the heroes who have inspired me throughout my life, one thing they universally never did is *give up*. They never forfeited what they wanted to achieve, and they never surrendered their dreams.

I want to summarize these principles for you in one place since they are critical to your ability to create what *you* want in life.

Principle 1: Get Clear. Knowing exactly what you want is the very first step. Without judgment or excuses, ask yourself what your ideal life would look like.

Principle 2: Set Goals. Whittle your dream down to realistic yet challenging goals and *write them down*.

Principle 3: Have a Plan. Good planning isn't a box ticking exercise. It starts with powerful questions, which then drive goal setting. Don't forget to have a solid financial plan in place, and always keep your priorities in mind.

Principle 4: Get Committed: You don't need to wait for motivation or inspiration. Take action, and *then* motivation will follow. There's no replacement for hard work—make it a habit!

Principle 5: Get Invested. Don't wait for others to invest in you; invest in yourself first. Be accountable to your goals and remember that *you* are always your most valuable asset.

Principle 6: Be Nice. Kindness does pay. Make everyone you meet feel important, and you will improve your life and career, not to mention your relationships.

Principle 7: Be Healed. When you heal your past and become whole, you make post-traumatic growth possible.

Principle 8: Get Out of Your Head. Identify your Saboteurs, and work to weaken them while you strengthen your highest self, your inner Sage. You have the power to rewrite the story of your life.

Principle 9: Own Your Truth. When you speak your truth, you can begin to live authentically and finally feel free. Embrace your story, release your shame, and don't be afraid to seek professional help.

Principle 10: Be Generous. Life becomes more meaningful when you shift your focus to what you can give instead of what you can get. One of the greatest things you can experience is the joy that comes from helping another human being.

Principle 11: Be Grateful. You can always do more, be more, and achieve your most ambitious dreams; but let that striving come from a place of appreciating just how blessed you already are.

YOU DID IT!

We've now reached the end of the book. Congratulations and well done!

Practice these principles and you will achieve the life you want. Master them and watch the miracles unfold in your life.

My questions for you now are: What will you do? What will you choose?

Your next step is completely up to you. I want to say one more time: the road map ahead is laid out, your dreams are achievable, and healing is possible—and you are only ever *One Decision Away.*

ACKNOWLEDGMENTS

———

"If I have seen further, it is by standing on the shoulders of giants."

—SIR ISAAC NEWTON, IN A LETTER TO ROBERT HOOKE 1675

I am deeply grateful for every person God led into my life to make this book a reality. Every conversation has given me the chance to dig deeper and find a common thread that connects all our different stories. I never knew how much sacrifice and work went into writing a book: endless days and nights spent researching, countless drafts, and plenty of prayer and patience. However, the experience is something I will carry with me for a lifetime.

I realize now that writing a great book takes more than just an idea but rather a deep sense of purpose. I'm so humbled that I've been able to create something to help others not only achieve their goals but to realize that fulfilment without healing from the past is impossible.

I've made many mistakes in my life. Having the courage to share "my truth" with you is a way for me to own every decision I've made, once and for all. I recognize that for many of you holding this book, the decisions I've made may not align with your values, and I respect that. But if I had not made those decisions, you would not be reading this book, I would not be who I am today, and I would not be so driven to help others who have traveled a similar path. This book is for them.

Writing this book would not have been possible without the support and understanding of my husband, Randy, and our two sons, Carlo and Enzo. Thank you, Randy, for staying by my side throughout this journey, and thank you for being one of the most reliable and honest people I know.

Thank you to my dear friends "my soul sisters" who have stayed by my side through thick and thin, always keeping my spirits up. Your friendship is a gift from heaven.

Plenty of people played a crucial role in my professional journey, and I want to take a moment to recognize them here:

Anthony Svach	Mary Terry
Dan Foslid	Matt Hostasa
David Junker	Michael Lewers
Doug Brewers	Mike Haglin
James Assali	Mike Tobin
Joe Devico	Paul Dolan
John Schiavone	Paul Kehrer
Lori Arrell	Rich Kozlowski
Mark McClure	Steve DeAngelis
Mark McGannon	Suzette Rothberg
Mary Jo Dickie	Thomas Pfeifer

I am eternally grateful to Paul Kehrer who gave me my first professional job opportunity in America, and for his wife, Esther, who took me in like a daughter. I have no idea where I'd be if Paul hadn't given me the opportunity that I so desperately needed at that time in my life.

I am also sincerely grateful to Doug Brewers who gave me my biggest career break. You took a chance on me, and I will never forget that.

I also want to thank and recognize those who I interviewed for this book. I sincerely hope that your insights, wisdom, and stories of courage will go on to inspire others, as they have inspired me:

Antwan Jackson	Jasna Burza
Britt Williams Baker	Kevin Bjerke
Galey Alix	Kimberly Neely
Gemma Naturkach	Josh Rudman

To all my coaching clients who allow me to do what I love: Thank you for letting me serve and guide you on your journeys.

To my aunt Grace and uncle Anthony, I have so much love and gratitude for you and everything you have done and meant to me.

Professor Eric Koester's author development process and coaching are extraordinary, and I am in awe of his willingness and ability to help authors execute their vision. I am grateful for his incredible team, including John Saunders, Brian Weiss, Amanda Brown, and Sherman Morrison.

To the publishing team at New Degree Press, who could not have been more helpful in guiding me in this process, thank you. I am deeply grateful to Michelle Pollack and Melody Delgado for their editorial help and patience.

Writing a book in English when you have never taken a formal English class is a humbling and surreal process. I'm forever indebted to Lyndsay Wilson for her ongoing support in helping me bring my stories to life. I have a legacy to pass on to my family for many generations because of her help, efforts, and encouragement.

I am grateful to all the financial advisors I've had the honor of serving as clients, and the colleagues I've worked alongside at these incredible companies I've been fortunate enough to represent: Ameriprise Financial, Morgan Stanley—Van Kampen, Goldman Sachs, and BlackRock. You gave me incredible opportunities to learn, grow, and build a life for myself and my family that I am very proud of.

A special thanks to those who have played the role of my mentors, coaches, and teachers in my journey, including:

Dr. Adam Grant	Jessica Gallo
Dr. Benjamin Hardy	Jim Stroker
Brandyn Negri	Joyce Salvo
Brenda Knap	Julie Gionet
Dr. Brené Brown	Kimberly Neeley
Charlotte Stallings	Michelle Keeley
Dayna Hopko	Mickey Carson
Deirdre Van Nest	Reese Berman
Doug Lennick	Dr. Shirzad Chamine
Jasna Burza	Dr. Tal Ben Shahar

I want to express gratitude to my grandmother, Maria, who did not give up on me, despite everything. She taught me to be strong, work hard, and have faith.

I am thankful to my birth mother, Helena, for bringing me into this world. She gave birth to me when she was just a teenager and had her share of life challenges, to say the very least. My grandmother did not think highly of my mother and her decisions, and I carried these stories of shame with me throughout my childhood. Though I carried those wounds for so long, I can now say I no longer bear that burden, and today I have nothing but gratitude for the woman who gave me life.

Her journey and my own reminds me that life is hard, but in the end, choosing forgiveness, healing, and growth is the only way forward into a better future for ourselves and for future generations.

My deepest gratitude goes to God and Jesus Christ. Without their unconditional love for me, independent of my actions, I would have felt completely lost, lonely, and hopeless. Thank you for being the constant presence in my life and for giving me everything I have.

For all of those who are hurting, unfilled, or trapped in bad relationships or unfulfilling careers; for all those living in shame; and for all those who have dreams to fulfill and goals to achieve; I want to say thank you for being the inspiration and reason why *One Decision Away* now exists.

I want to apologize if by reading this book you've learned things about me that I haven't been entirely honest about. As I mentioned before, I have made many mistakes, but I am striving every day to live in truth. All I can say now is that I hope you can find forgiveness in your heart. I am grateful for the opportunity you gave me to be part of your journey, in whatever way.

My vision is that this book will impact countless lives, both personally and professionally. I believe in my heart that the best days are still ahead of us. We have barely touched our true potential. What a joy and honor to be part of that journey!

A special thank you to these angels I believe God placed in my life. Your support and love have changed my life:

Alexandre de Paula Melo   Keala Pellegrino
Bonnie Stanley   Loren Balfour
Carmem Siviero   Mara and Michele Filippi
Claudio Trabulsi   Marlete Assunção
Dona Helena   Sylvia DeMott
Dona Maria and Sr. Jose   Patricia de Paiva Medeiros
Doroff Family   Paulo Vasconcelos
Fernando de Souza   Roberta Filippi
Ginger Shoemaker   Thais de Melo
Jasmine Hornbrook   Tia Rosa
Julia Catarina de Souza

I want to express deep appreciation for the important feedback I received from my beta readers, which helped me bring the most important messages to my readers and keep me focused as I wrote and revised the book. Lastly, thank you to everyone who pre-ordered the book and helped spread the word. Your efforts have made possible a book I am sincerely proud of. I am grateful for all your help.

Aimee Ballou
Alan Ng
Alex and Claudia Savelli
Aline Condon
Alisa Lamont
Alisa Maute
Alyssa Thomas *
Amalia Fattori
Amber Lynn Hutton
Amy Howe
Anamaria Betterman
Andrew Schurle
Andreza Benke Derevyanko
Anelisa Pontes
Angela Gantt
Angela Junker
Angela Kralovec
Angela Librizzi
Angie Colliander **
Anna Morgan
Anna Rusk
Anne Brooks
Anne Kinsman *
Anthony Schulzetenberg
Arthur Oliver *
Baharak Pezeshki
Becky Fellbaum
Becky Watson

Ben Sjodin
Beth Wills
Betsy Kelly
Bilal Little
Bill Rothschild
Bill and Jane Williams *
Bonnie Stanley *
Brad Napoli
Brandyn Negri
Brent Love *
Brent Trentham
Brett Mossman
Brian Muller
Brian O'Connell
Bridget Reber
Bryan Sweet
Candice Tse *
Carl and Lesley Quaglia
Carla Dahl
Carlo Doroff *
Caroline Bavis
Carrie Drinkwine **
Cat Breet
Chad Dziedzic *
Chase La Vine
Cherie Peterson *
Chris Bisaillon
Chris Wheeler Doe

Christine Bruno
Christine Gaffron
Christopher Davis
C.J. Nesher
Colleen Wolfe
Courtney Costigan
Courtney Nuness
Courtney Walls
Craig Jergenson
Craig Olson
Cristiana Ercoli
Dan Arrell
Dana Brewer
Danielle Lore
Darren Griffiths
David Purdy
Dawn Dahlby
Dawn Scholl
Dean Silverman
Deirdre Van Nest **
Denise Palmer
Deniz Franke
Devon Brazil
Diana M. Geller
Diana Rosemberg
Diane Svoboda
Dolly Bilyeu
Doug Bogie
Doug Brewers **
Ed Mathie
Elizabeth Jensen
Elizabeth Koehler **

Elizabeth Stokes
Enzo Doroff *
Eric Koester **
Ericka Miller
Erin Brady
Erin Zosel
Esther and Paul Kehrer **
Eva Balint
Fabiana Peterson
Flavia Erickson *
Gary Schwartz *
Geetu Sharma
Gemma Naturkach **
George Papadoyannis
Gerardo G. Aguilera
Giovanna Filippi Del Nero
G.J. Lempe
Glynne Bassi *
Greg Prokott *
Gregory R. Hoehn
Hannah Fleming
Heather Croke *
Heather Edelson
Heather Fredrickson
Heloiza Mendes
Ingrid Christensen **
Irene Kelly
Izzy Chang
Jaci Enberg
Jake Wilson
James Assali and
Michael Mauch *

James J. Beste *
Jamie O'Rourke
Jamie Ward
Janet Doroff
Jasmine Hornbrook *
Jasmine Stringer *
Jasna Burza *
Jason Stevens
Jason Tamminen
Jay Beaulieu
Jill Bergerud
Jeff and Roberta Hohbach *
Jeff Van Keulen
Jen Colburn
Jenna Dubuc
Jenni Flores
Jennifer Foster
Jennifer Stevens
Jeremy Blubaugh
Jesse Tordsen
Jessica Fields
Jessica Gallo *
Jessica Kelly
Jessica Lydia Skilar
Jessica Nickelson
Jessica Rogers
Jilene Framke
Jill and Patrick Haspert
Jill Lawrence *
Jim Cavalier *
Jodee Kozlak **
Jodi Short

John Lyons
John Reamer *
John Schiavone
John Stadtmueller
Jolaine Beddow-Beste
Joseph Balestra *
Joseph Caldwell
Josh Ely
Josh Rudman *
Julia Knapp
Juliana Batista
Juliana Panetta
Julie Maeyaert *
Julie Phaxay
Julie Spangler *
Julie Tanaka
June Sonsalla
Justin Bieganek *
Kari Douglas Ehleringer
Kari Erickson *
Karl Pawlowski
Karolin Lex
Kate Damato
Katelyn VanHeel
Katie and Eddie Kaiser
Katie Swimley
Katie Ware
Katya Zitzer
Kelly Perry *
Kelly Apple
Kelsey Zwiebel *
Kendall Stark

Kendra Ryder
Keri Gawlik
Kevin Bjerke **
Kimberly A. Maciej *
Kimberly Bolz-Andolshek
Kimberly Cavalcante
Kimberly Mickelson *
Kimberly Neely **
Koren Nelson
Kris Petersen
Kristin Bilden
Kristin Rognerud
Kristine Bisanz
Kristine Cotroneo
Lalita Zapata
Lance Butner *
Laura Horton
Laura Mcgill
Laura Miller
Laura Nardone
Laurel Johnson *
Lauren McFadden
Lea Gallop *
Leisa Olson
Lenita Benke
Leslie Cadle *
Leslie Finnoff
Leslie Richard
Lili Hall *
Linda Zimmerman *
Lindsay Swiggum
Lindsay Ardis

Lisa M. Christianson *
Lisa M. Jendro
Lisa Tuttle
Loni Harris
Loren Kamrin Balfour **
Lorena and Patrick Assali
Lorenzo Bassi
Lori Arrell *
Lou Welter
Luciana Verhoye Passeri
Maia Wright
Marcie Mueller
Maria Gans
Maria Johnson
Mariam Vedadi *
Mariana Quiroga
Marie Elena Rigo *
Marisa Andert
Mark and Emily Joern
Mark Pearson
Mark Theis
Mary and Todd Doroff
Matt Hostasa
Matt Wolff
Matthew Adey *
Matthew Kurland
Meg Jakubik
Megan Knudson
Megan Rebholtz
Melisa Lopez Franzen
Melissa Lizotte
Meta Webb

Michael Branch *
Michael Fink
Michael H. Lewers
Michael Metzger
Michael Ricci
Michael Tobin *
Michele Hanson *
Michelle Athmann
Michelle Campbell
Michelle Gans *
Michelle Glood
Michelle Keeley **
Michelle Lewis
Michelle Thomas
Michelle Young
Mike Cassidy *
Mike Miller
Mike Wade
Mikki Johnson
Molly Gaines *
Monica Wilinski
Monique Werry **
Morgan Jaros *
Nancy Eserkaln
Nassim Rossi
Neesha Kurian *
Nicholas Adams
Nicholette Schlaeger
Nicole Williams
Oscar Pulido
Oscar Sanchez Christensen
Pat Furlong

Patricia Boettner
Patricia Kendrick
Patty Groff
Paul Singh
Paul and Kathleen Sylvester *
Paula and Jeff Costa Bravo
Paula Meyer
Pete and Terrie Silbaugh *
Rachel Formantes
Randy Doroff **
Randy Ehleringer
Raquel Araujo *
Rebecca Sorensen
Renee Langlois *
Richard Schultz *
Rick Golod
Rob Fakhry
Robert and Sarah Hackett
Robert Bonine **
Robert Kron
Rodney Meyer
Roseanne Hope *
Roxanne May
Sandra Larson
Sarah Basile
Sarah Kjellberg
Scott Maeyaert
Scott Nelson
Sean McDermott
Shannon Chamberlain
Shannon Rusk *
Sharon Hayman

Sheila Milton
Sherry Richgels *
Stacy Bednar
Stefani Gerczak *
Stefanie Tschida
Stephani Sundry
Stephanie Pierce
Stephanie Tennessen
Stephanie and Mike Greene
Stephen Kingsley
Stephen Witthuhn
Steve Deacon
Steve Passeri
Suzanne Holt
Sydney Eckhart
Sydney Holly
Sylvia DeMott *
Tamrah O'Neil
Tanya Boigenzahn
Terri Peterson

Terry Huddle
Theodore Enders
Thomas Antonovich *
Thomas and Tammy Pfeifer **
Tiffany Tobias *
Tim Hsu
Tim and Katie Miller *
Tim Ott
Tobbie Walter
Todd and Jennifer Johnson
Tom Endersbe
Tom Gartner
Trevor Dunn
Trisha London *
Troy Brueggemeier
Tyson Ray **
Veronica and Scott Doroff
Wendy Reiss
Whit Raymond
William Shannon

* Special Recognition
** Extra Special Recognition

APPENDIX

INTRODUCTION

BrainyMedia Inc. "Oliver Wendell Holmes, Sr. Quotes." 2022.
https://www.brainyquote.com/quotes/oliver_wendell_holmes_
sr_104426.

Cook, I. "Who Is Driving the Great Resignation?" *Harvard Business
Review*, September 15, 2021.
https://hbr.org/2021/09/who-is-driving-the-great-resignation.

Gallup Organization. 2022. *U.S. State of the Global Workplace: 2022
Report*. Washington, DC: Gallup Organization.
https://www.gallup.com/workplace/349484/state-of-the-global-
workplace-2022-report.aspx.

National Alliance of Mental Illness (NAMI), "Mental Health by the
Numbers," Nami.org. February 2022,
https://www.nami.org/mhstats.

Santomauro, Damian F., Ana M. Mantilla Herrera, Jamileh Shadid, Peng zheng, Charlie Ashbaugh, David M. Pigott, Cristiana Abbafati, Cristopher Adolph, Joanna O. Amlag, Alexandr Aravkin Y., et. al. (Covid-19 Mental Disorders Collaborators.) "Global Prevalence and Burden of Depressive and Anxiety Disorders in 204 Countries and Territories in 2020 Due to the COVID-19 Pandemic." *The Lancet* 398, no. 10312 (2021) https://doi.org/10.1016/S0140-6736(21)02143-7.

US Department of Health and Human Services. Centers for Disease Control and Prevention (CDC). *Anxiety and Depression Household Pulse Survey.* Accessed 3 June 2022. https://www.cdc.gov/about/history/.

CHAPTER 1

Byrne, Rhonda. *The Secret.* Simon and Schuster, 2006.

Coelho, Paulo. "The 3 Symptoms of Killing Our Dreams." *Paulo Coelho Stories and Reflections* (blog), 26 April 2022. https://paulocoelhoblog.com/2020/11/20/our-dream/.

Covey, Stephen R. *The 7 Habits of Highly Effective People: Revised and Updated: 30th Anniversary Edition.* New York: Simon and Schuster, 2020.

Lazenby, Roland. *Michael Jordan: The Life.* Back Bay Books, 2015.

Loder, Vanessa. "What Entrepreneurs Can Learn from Olympic athletes." *Forbes*, July 23, 2014. https://www.forbes.com/sites/vanessaloder/2014/07/23/the-power-of-vision-what-entrepreneurs-can-learn-from-olympic-athletes/?sh=59c0cf0e6e74.

Ranganathan, Vinoth K., Vlodek Siemionow, Jing Z. Liu, Vinod Sahgal, and Guang H. Yue. "From Mental Power to Muscle Power—Gaining Strength by Using the Mind." *Neuropsychologia* 42, no. 7 (2004): 944–56. 10.1016/j. neuropsychologia.2003.11.018.

Smith, Will, and Mark Manson. *Will*. London: Penguin Press, 2021.

CHAPTER 2

Acton, Annabel. "How to Set Goals (And Why You Should Write Them Down)." *Forbes*, November 3, 2017. https://www.forbes.com/sites/annabelacton/2017/11/03/how-to-set-goals-and-why-you-should-do-it/?sh=7f316555162d.

Collins, Jim, and Jerry I. Porras. *Built to Last: Successful Habits of Visionary Companies*. New York: Harper Business, 1994.

Dominican University of California. "Study Focuses on Strategies for Achieving Goals, Resolutions." Dominican University of California press release, 2 January, 2015. https://scholar.dominican.edu/cgi/viewcontent. cgi?article=1265&context=news-releases.

Doran, George T. "There's a S.M.A.R.T. Way to Write Management's Goals and Objectives". *Management Review* 70, no. 11 (1981): 35–36.

Jacoby, Larry L. "On Interpreting the Effects of Repetition: Solving a Problem Versus Remembering a Solution." *Journal of Verbal Learning and Verbal Behavior* 17, no. 6 (1978): 649–668. doi:10.1016/S0022-5371(78)90393-6.

Salmon-Stephens, Tammy. "Meet Pact: The Goal Setting Technique You've Never Heard Of." *National Society of Leadership and Success* (blog), January 25, 2021. https://www.nsls.org/blog/pact-goal-setting-technique.

Savara, Sid. "Writing Down Your Goals – The Harvard Written Goal Study. Fact or Fiction?" *Sid Savara* (blog), 26 April 2022. https://sidsavara.com/fact-or-fiction-the-truth-about-the-harvard-written-goal-study/.

CHAPTER 3

Board of Governors of the Federal Reserve System. *Report on the Economic Well-Being of U.S Households in 2019.* Washington: Printing and Fulfilment, 2019. 26 April 2022. https://www.federalreserve.gov/publications/files/2018-report-economic-well-being-us-households-201905.pdf.

Dalio, Ray. *Principles: Life and Work.* New York: Simon and Schuster, 2021.

Dahlby, Dawn. "Live Wellthy," 2022. https://dawndahlby.com/.

Janes, Dow. 2022.
https://dowjanes.com/.

Go Banking Rates. "64% of Americans Aren't Prepared for Retirement — and 48% Don't Care." 2019.
https://www.gobankingrates.com/retirement/planning/why-americans-will-retire-broke/.

Lekushoff, Matthew. "Things I've Learnt from Ray Dalio." *Matthew Lekushoff* (blog), 20 January 2021.
https://www.matthewlekushoff.ca/matthews-blog/2021/01/20/things-ive-learned-from-ray-dalio-life-version?sc_lang=en.

National Endowment for Financial Education. *Overconfident and Underprepared: The Disconnect Between Millennials and Their Money Insights from the 2015 National Financial Capability Study.* Colorado: NEFE, 2022.
https://www.nefe.org/_images/research/GWU-Financial-Capability-Young-Adults/GWU-Financial-Capability-Young-Adults-Research-Brief.pdf.

Robbins, Tony. "Ask Better Questions. The 3 Questions That Will Completely Reframe Your Daily Life Experiences." *Tony Robbins* (blog), 26 April.
https://www.tonyrobbins.com/mind-meaning/ask-better-questions/.

Schwab, Charles. "Schwab Modern Wealth Survey Reveals Americans' Changing Priorities around Spending, Saving and Mental Health." 2021.
https://www.aboutschwab.com/modern-wealth-survey-2021.

Shiels, Maggie. "A Chat with the Man behind Mobiles." *BBC,* 21 April, 2003. http://news.bbc.co.uk/1/hi/uk/2963619.stm.

The Economist Staff. "Father of the Cell Phone." *Economist*, June 4, 2009. https://www.economist.com/technology-quarterly/2009/06/06/father-of-the-cell-phone.

Weisul, Kimberly. "It Doesn't Pay to Be Nice. Here's How Much It Costs." *CBS News,* August 7, 2011. https://www.cbsnews.com/news/it-doesnt-pay-to-be-nice-this-is-how-much-it-costs/.

CHAPTER 4

BrainyMedia Inc. "Maria Bartiromo Quotes." 2022. https://www.brainyquote.com/quotes/maria_bartiromo_252502, accessed May 19, 2022.

Gallup Organization. 2022. *U.S. State of the Global Workplace: 2022 Report*. Washington, DC: Gallup Organization. https://www.gallup.com/workplace/349484/state-of-the-global-workplace-2022-report.aspx.

Leonhardt, Megan. "The Great Resignation Rages on as a Record 4.5 Million Americans Quit." *Fortune*, January 4, 2022. https://fortune.com/2022/01/04/great-resignation-record-quit-rate-4-5-million/.

Schnall, Marianne. "The Huffington Post Exclusive: Interview with Oprah about Her School for Girls." *The Huffington Post*, December 2017. https://www.huffpost.com/entry/oprah-school-for-girls_b_1959271.

CHAPTER 5

247 Motivation. "Les Brown - The Greatest Advice Ever Told | Powerful Motivational Video 2021." 2021. Video, 31.26. https://www.youtube.com/watch?v=pIDNCqExjI0&ab_channel=247Motivation.

Fogg, Brian Jeffrey. *Tiny Habits: The Small Changes That Change Everything*. Boston: Mariner Books, 2021.

Lane, Randall. "Warren Buffett: My Greatest Investing Advice and the Investments Everyone Should Make." *Forbes*, September 20, 2017. https://www.forbes.com/sites/randalllane/2017/09/20/warren-buffett-my-greatest-investing-advice-and-the-investments-everyone-should-make/?sh=f356717593ea.

Newland, Stephen. "The Power of Accountability." *AFCPE The Standard Newsletter* (blog), 3rd quarter 2018. https://www.afcpe.org/news-and-publications/the-standard/2018-3/the-power-of-accountability/.

Success staff. "Jim Rohn on Working Harder on Yourself Than on Your Job." *Success*, August 24, 2017. https://www.success.com/jim-rohn-on-working-harder-on-yourself-than-your-job/.

Wick, Doug. "Pearson's Law." *Positioning Systems Blog* (blog), December 15, 2008. http://positioningsystems.com/blog.php?entryID=67.

CHAPTER 6

Gray, Kurt, Adrian F. Ward, and Michael I. Norton. "Paying It Forward: Generalized Reciprocity and the Limits of Generosity." *Journal of Experimental Psychology: General* 143, no. 1 (2014): 247–54. 10.1037/a0031047.

Investment News Staff. "2021 Women in Asset Management Awards." *Investment News,* November 1, 2021. https://www.investmentnews.com/2021-women-in-asset-management-awards-213467.

Kravetz, Dennis J. *The Human Resources Revolution: Implementing Progressive Management Practices for Bottom-Line Success (Jossey Bass Business & Management Series)*. Switzerland: Pfeiffer, 1988.

Sloma, Richard, S. *The Turnaround Manager's Handbook.* Maryland: Beard Books, 2000.

Thaler, Linda Kaplan, and Robin Koval. *The Power of Nice: How to Conquer the Business World with Kindness.* London: Virgin Publishing, 2006.

CHAPTER 7

Ben-Shahar, Tal. "Let's Suffer from Posttraumatic Growth." *The Art of Whole Being* (blog), *Psychology Today*, July 7, 2020. https://www.psychologytoday.com/us/blog/the-art-whole-being/202007/let-s-suffer-post-traumatic-growth.

Evans, Melanie T. "How Childhood Trauma Makes Us Susceptible to Narcissists." *Melanie Tonia Evans* (blog), 26 April, 2022. https://blog.melanietoniaevans.com/how-childhood-trauma-makes-us-susceptible-to-narcissists/.

Fox, Emmet. *The Wonder Child*. Wisconsin: Literary Licensing, 2011.

Hanh, Thich Nhat. *Reconciliation: Healing the Inner Child*. California: Parallax Press, 2006.

Lindley, Jennifer K. "What Is Resilience? Psychologists Explain How to Grow from Painful Moments." *Health*, June 25, 2020. https://www.health.com/condition/stress/how-to-heal-and-grow-from-our-toughest-moments.

Seery, Mark D., E. Alison Holman, and Roxane C. Silver. "Whatever Does Not Kill Us: Cumulative Lifetime Adversity, Vulnerability, and Resilience." *Journal of Personality and Social Psychology*, 99, no. 6 (2010): 1025–41. https://doi.org/10.1037/a0021344.

Walker, Hannah E., Jennifer S. Freud, Robin A. Ellis, Shawn M. Fraine, and Laura C. Wilson. "The Prevalence of Sexual Revictimization: A Meta-Analytic Review." *Trauma, Violence, & Abuse* 20, no. 1 (2017): 67–80. 10.1177/1524838017692364.

CHAPTER 8

Chamine, Shirzad. *Positive Intelligence: Why Only 20% of Teams and Individuals Achieve Their True Potential and How You Can Achieve Yours.* Texas: Greenleaf Book Group Press, 2012.

Clance, Pauline R., and Suzanne A. Imes. "The Imposter Phenomenon in High Achieving Women: Dynamics and Therapeutic Intervention." *Psychotherapy: Theory, Research & Practice* 15, no. 3 (1978): 241–7. https://doi.org/10.1037/h0086006.

Leahy, Robert L. *The Worry Cure.* Pennsylvania: Harmony, 2005.

Ludden, Jennifer. "Sotomayor: 'Always Looking Over My Shoulder'." *NPR*, May 26, 2009. https://www.npr.org/2009/05/26/104538436/sotomayor-always-looking-over-my-shoulder?t=1652965029312.

Michael Shermer, "The Pattern behind Self-Deception," filmed February 2010 in Longbeach California. TED Video, 18:45, https://www.ted.com/talks/michael_shermer_the_pattern_behind_self_deception?language=en.

Taleb, Nicholas. *The Black Swan: The Impact of the Highly Improbable.* New York: Random House Publishing, 2010.

Tseng, Julie, and Jordan Poppenk. "Brain Meta-State Transitions Demarcate Thoughts across Task Contexts Exposing the Mental Noise of Trait Neuroticism." *Nature Communications* 11, no. 3480 (2020). https://doi.org/10.1038/s41467-020-17255-9.

CHAPTER 9

Brown, Brené. *Daring Greatly: How the Courage to Be Vulnerable Transforms the Way We Live, Love, Parent, and Lead.* New York City: Avery, 2015.

Brown, Brené. "Shame Resilience Theory: A Grounded Theory Study on Women and Shame." *Families in Society* 87, no. 1 (2006): 43–52.
https://doi.org/10.1606/1044-3894.3483.

Mayer, Claude-Hélène. "Shame—'A Soul Feeding Emotion': Archetypal Work and the Transformation of the Shadow of Shame in a Group Development Process." In *The Value of Shame. Exploring a Health Resource in Cultural Contexts,* edited by Elisabeth Vanderheiden and Claude-Hélène Mayer, pp. 277–302. New York: Springer, 2017.

Prevost, Chad, and Shelley Prevost. "How to Live In Your Truth: The Difference between Personal Values and Social Conditioning." *Big Self School* (blog), 26 April 2022.
https://www.bigselfschool.com/post/how-to-live-in-your-truth.

Sheldon, Kennon M. "Becoming Oneself: The Central Role of Self-Concordant Goal Selection." *Personality and Social Psychology Review* 18, no. 4 (2014): 349–65.
https://doi.org/10.1177/1088868314538549.

CHAPTER 10

Anderson, Kare. "Pay It Forward with a Five-Minute Favor." *Forbes*, July 17, 2013. https://www.forbes.com/sites/kareanderson/2013/07/17/pay-it-forward-with-the-five-minute-favor/?sh=6d11f8f36f5d.

Ben-Shahar, Tal. *Choosing the Life You Want: The Path to Conscious Happiness*. New York: The Experiment LLC, 2014.

Dunn, Elizabeth W., Lara B. Aknin, and Michael I. Norton. "Spending Money on Others Promotes Happiness." *Science* 319, no. 5870 (2008): 1687–8. 10.1126/science.1150952.

Fowler, James H., and Nicholas A. Christakis. "Cooperative Behavior Cascades in Human Social Networks." *Proceedings of the National Academy of Sciences* 107, no. 12 (2010): 5334–8. https://doi.org/10.1073/pnas.0913149107.

Gates, Bill, and Melinda Gates. "10 Tough Questions We Get Asked." *Gates Notes* (blog), February 13, 2018. https://www.gatesnotes.com/2018-Annual-Letter?WT. mc_id=02_13_2018_02_AnnualLetter2018_BG-media_&WT. tsrc=BGmedia.

Grant, Adam. *Give and Take: Why Helping Others Drives Our Success*. London: Penguin Books, 2014.

Horst, Peter. "BlackRock CEO Tells Companies to Contribute to Society. Here's Where to Start." *Forbes*, January 16, 2018. https://www.forbes.com/sites/peterhorst/2018/01/16/blackrock-ceo-tells-companies-to-contribute-to-society-heres-where-to-start/?sh=3371c7b9971d.

Moll, Jorge, Frank Krueger, Roland Zahn, Mattheo Pardini, Ricardo de Oliveira-Souza, and Jordan Grafman. "Human Fronto-mesolimbic Networks Guide Decisions about Charitable Donation." *Proceedings of the National Academy of Sciences of the United States of America* 103, no. 42 (2006): 15623–8. doi:10.1073/pnas.0604475103.

Piferi, Rachel L., and Kathleen A. Lawler. "Social Support and Ambulatory Blood Pressure: An Examination of Both Receiving and Giving." *International Journal of Psychophysiology* 62, no. 2 (2006): 328–36. 10.1016/j.ijpsycho.2006.06.002.

Podsakoff, Nathan P., Steven W. Whiting, Phillip Podsakoff, and Brian D. Blume. "Individual- and Organizational-Level Consequences of Organizational Citizenship Behaviors: A Meta-Analysis." *Journal of Applied Psychology* 94, no. 1 (2009): 122–41. 10.1037/a0013079.

CHAPTER 11

Burke, Ronald J., Eddy S. Ng, and Lisa Fiksenbaum. "Virtues, Work Satisfactions and Psychological Wellbeing among Nurses." *International Journal of Workplace Health Management* 2 (2009): 202–219. 10.1108/17538350910993403.

Emmons, Robert A., and Michael E. McCullough. *Highlights from the Research Project on Gratitude and Thankfulness.* California: Robert Emmons, 26 April, 2022. https://citeseerx.ist.psu.edu/viewdoc/download?doi=10.1.1.520.4351&rep=rep1&type=pdf.

Emmons, Roger A. "Why Gratitude Is Good." *Greater Good Magazine*, November 16, 2010. https://greatergood.berkeley.edu/article/item/why_gratitude_is_good.

Mann, Annamarie, and Nate Dvorak. Gallup Organization. 2016. *Employee Recognition: Low Cost; High Impact.* Washington, DC: Gallup Organization. https://www.gallup.com/workplace/236441/employee-recognition-low-cost-high-impact.aspx.

Sullivan, Dan, and Benjamin Hardy. *The Gap and the Gain: The High Achievers' Guide to Happiness, Confidence, and Success.* California: Hay House Business, 2021.

Sullivan, Dan. "The Best Goal-Measurement Strategy for Entrepreneurs." *Strategic Coach* (blog), 7 June 2022. https://resources.strategiccoach.com/search?ufq=the%20gap&ufs=1539081.

Waitzkin, Josh. *The Art of Learning: An Inner Journey to Optimal Performance.* New York: Free Press, 2008.

Wood, Alex M., Stephen Joseph, and John Maltby. "Gratitude Predicts Psychological Well-Being above the Big Five Facets." *Personality and Individual Differences* 46, no. 4 (2009): 443–7. 10.1016/j.paid.2008.11.012.

CPSIA information can be obtained
at www.ICGtesting.com
Printed in the USA
BVHW032214201022
649968BV00007B/17/J